The Sneaky Chef:

How to Cheat on Your Man
(In the Kitchen)

Praise for *The Sneaky Chef*:

"Contains realistic ways to boost nutrition in children's diets."
—*Publishers Weekly*

"A fun approach to sneaking."
—Elouise Parker, *New York Daily News*

"A brilliant and timely concept."
—Chef Daniel Boulud

"[Lapine] appears to have struck a cultural and medical chord."
—Kathleen Ryan O'Connor, *The Journal News*

"Lapine has some great ideas, including recipes for make-ahead purees,
one of her secret weapons."
—Claudia Zapata, *San Antonio Express-News*

"Lots of good ideas and recipes that will work for you if you are
at your wits end...and even if you're not."
—Vicki Lansky, author of *Feed Me, I'm Yours*

The Sneaky Chef:

How to Cheat on Your Man (In the Kitchen)

Hiding Healthy Foods in Hearty Meals

Any Guy Will Love

BY MISSY CHASE LAPINE

RUNNING PRESS
PHILADELPHIA • LONDON

© 2008 by Missy Chase Lapine

All rights reserved under the Pan-American and International Copyright Conventions

Printed in the United States

This book may not be reproduced in whole or in part, in any form or by any means, electronic or mechanical, including photocopying, recording, or by any information storage and retrieval system now known or hereafter invented, without written permission from the publisher.

9   8   7   6   5   4   3   2   1

Digit on the right indicates the number of this printing

Library of Congress Control Number: 2008920405

ISBN: 978-0-7624-3320-9

Cover design by Bill Jones
Interior design by Alicia Freile
Edited by Jennifer Kasius
Nutritionist: Shoshana Werber, MS, RD, CDN
Author photo by Scott Calman
Food photography by Jerry Errico
Food styling by Brian Preston-Campbell
Logo by Kristopher Weber
Typography: Frutiger, Garth Graphic and Sassoon

Running Press Book Publishers
2300 Chestnut Street
Philadelphia, PA 19103-4371

Visit us on the web!
www.runningpress.com

*This book is dedicated
to my husband and best friend, Rick Lapine,
and to our girls, Samantha and Emily.*

Table of Contents

Lunch Pail Recipes

Dinner

On the Grill

Halftime Snacks

Drinks (Non-Alcoholic)

Alcoholic Drinks

Desserts

Acknowledgments 338

Index 341

Foreword

Lori Mosca, M.D., M.P.H., Ph.D.

Lin Yutang said "Our lives are not in the lap of the gods, but in the lap of our cooks." Diet is one of the most powerful weapons we have against heart disease and many other chronic conditions, yet many myths surround nutrition and health—and one of them is that if something tastes good then it must be bad for you. Not true! Another myth is that eating well is all work and no fun. Not so! The truth is that food *should* be fun—that eating should be a relaxed and pleasurable experience. All too often recommendations for healthy lifestyle change are perceived to be restrictive or are

a set up for failure over the long term. A simple solution is to view eating as a way of life— not a diet—and to take an approach to food that allows us to "have our cake and eat it too." What Missy Chase Lapine gives us is exactly that. She magically transforms some of men's favorite foods into healthier versions the *Sneaky Chef* way. In doing so, she has created a real-life tool to help in sustaining lifestyle changes over the long haul.

Every day, I see the correlation between poor lifestyle choices and heart disease. No one is ever too young to start thinking about CVD—cardiovascular disease—which is responsible for nearly half of all deaths in the United States. Too many men don't take this matter seriously until they are scared to death. By that time, they have to overcome the damage from years of poor choices and poor nutrition. Several factors contribute to CVD, but I believe the root cause for most people is lifestyle. While genetics can also play a role, our genes don't have to determine our destiny. By not smoking, getting regular physical activity, eating well, and maintaining a healthy weight, we can go a long way to protect ourselves, and our men.

Where diet is concerned, the prescription pantry would look something like the master shopping list in this book: oats, blueberries, walnuts, sardines, pomegranate juice, whole grains, fruits, veggies, onions, garlic, cumin, cinnamon, and lean protein. And it would omit foods high in saturated or trans fats, refined sugar, and full-fat dairy. I often tell my patients if a food doesn't come from the ground, a tree, or the sea, you shouldn't eat it except on rare occasions.

As a doctor, wife, and mother of two sons, I'm well aware that such prescriptions are easier to write than to follow (even among my medical colleagues who know better).

All too often, life gets in the way of our good intentions. Unfortunately, I have seen that attempts at restructuring lifestyles often fail simply because of the stress, time constraints, and demands of our everyday lives. What we need are creative and practical solutions to engage in healthy lifestyles and prepare attractive and great-tasting meals. *The Sneaky Chef* is a huge leap forward in helping us move beyond the ordinary to begin to live and experience the extraordinary. Missy has given us a *tantalizing* solution that can transform our kitchens and our lives. Enjoy!

Lori Mosca, M.D., M.P.H., Ph.D., is Director of Preventive Cardiology at New York-Presbyterian Hospital, and is Associate Professor of Medicine at Columbia University Medical Center. Dr. Mosca founded and is Director of the Columbia Center for Heart Disease Prevention in midtown Manhattan. She is author of *Heart to Heart: A Personal Plan for Creating a Heart-Healthy Family*, published by HCI Books.

CHAPTER ONE

Eat, Drink—And Live to Tell About It

"Chili represents your three stages of matter:

solid, liquid, and eventually, gas."

—Roseanne Barr

This book is the inadvertent by-product of my first book, *The Sneaky Chef: Simple Strategies for Hiding Healthy Foods in Kids' Favorite Meals*. Pretty early on in the process of testing recipes for the children's book, I realized that my husband, Rick, was eating healthier than ever before, because he was being given the same meals I fed the kids. He was chowing down on healthy foods he never would have gone near in their undisguised state—but since they were "hiding" in food he liked, he had no problem with them.

For some time, I had been holding on to my little bag of tricks—methods for sneaking vegetables, whole grains, beans, and fruit into my family's meals—like state secrets, because I didn't want the kids to know what I'd been doing. All you have to do with children is hint that an ingredient is healthy and they'll make a face. After a while, though, I figured it was time to reveal my handiwork to the adult at the table who was also being fooled.

But I was wrong. Once Rick was in on the tricks, he started showing resistance, refusing to eat certain dishes, and complaining about not liking this vegetable or that healthy grain or bean! I should have known better. After all, this is a guy who never tasted a plum until he was forty, and then only because I relentlessly coaxed him into trying this "foreign fruit." Now he loves plums, but he still won't knowingly try other foods that are outside of his comfort zone.

So I decided to stop telling my husband every little detail of what I was up to, and I went back to keeping my recipes to myself. Lo and behold, he started eating nearly everything I served again.

In some ways, men are a lot like kids. Here are just a few of the stories I collected when interviewing people for this book:

Lilah

My grandfather was a gracious and wise gentleman in every way, but he hated all vegetables. Whenever he was presented with them at a meal, he would politely refuse by saying, "No thank you, never on a Monday." If he happened to be dining with you on a Tuesday, he would simply say, "No thank you, never on a Tuesday." It didn't matter how often Grandma would tell him that his body needed the veggies; he seemed to think he was excused because it was the wrong day of the week.

Sharon

My husband, Jeff, once read that alcohol dissolves fat. Therefore, he believes that so long as he is drinking red wine with his meal, he can eat whatever he wants. He has gone on to classify virtually all alcohol as "healthy," based on the "garnish principle": a martini is a "healthy" drink because it has an olive or onion in it, and a piña colada is good for you because it's served with a slice of pineapple. Of course, any drink that uses cranberry juice as a mixer improves your health on contact. When I pressed him on eating his vegetables the other day, he retorted, "Why would I have to? I'm having a Bloody Mary, which is every bit a member of the salad family."

Stacey

My husband insists that none of the foods on his plate can touch one another. The only "vegetables" he eats are French fries and ketchup, and he's quite sure that satisfies the government's minimum requirement. He's actually making our two small children pickier eaters than they were before!

Kathy

My boyfriend predominantly eats from two food groups: sugar and lard, and he sincerely believes that popcorn is a vegetable. The worst part is, he's thin, so he thinks he can get away with it. He's still in his early thirties, so he can keep up the illusion for another ten years or so, but I'm nervous about the future with him.

Robyn

Bill will only eat white or brown foods. No color. As a fashion philosophy this isn't a bad plan, but it's not so ideal for a health plan. Tonight I watched him meticulously pick out every last veggie from his plate. One night I gave in to having pizza for dinner, but there was a catch: broccoli was the topping. The kids were furious, but they reluctantly ate it; Bill picked it off with his fingers, as if he was eliminating dust balls.

I swear an oath that I did not make these up. As you can see, some men have irrational aversions that can't be argued away with logical thought. There are certain foods that they "hate," and they'll do anything to avoid them, no matter what. Even if they last had asparagus when they were five and found it disgusting because their mothers burned it, they're still convinced that asparagus is despicable. These men avoid new foods at all costs and associate the word *healthy* with *yucky*. There are foods, usually those their mothers gave them to make them happy or to disrupt their temper tantrums, that they associate with comfort, and they'll turn to them in times of stress. These men are certain that they'll still be hungry after eating a vegetarian meal. And finally, just like kids, these men don't like being told what to do.

I love my husband dearly, but I could fill this entire first chapter with stories about his eating eccentricities. I think Rick is far more concerned with avoiding what he dislikes than with eating what he likes. If he says he hates sardines, then he won't go near them, even under threat of death. Here are a few more examples:

- Eggs are okay in an omelet (never scrambled!), but only if the omelet is served "pancake" style (never folded!) and burned beyond recognition.
- Carrots are okay, but only raw, absolutely never cooked.
- Cauliflower is so bad that as a child, he used to leave the house when his mother cooked it.
- He will allow my mother to visit only if she signs an affidavit saying that she will not open a can of sardines if he is anywhere near the kitchen.

I could keep going, but that wouldn't be fair to my father, who is the original picky adult male.

When I asked my dad to help me with this book by talking about his own reluctance to eat vegetables, he clarified for me, "Sweetheart, I just have certain *epicurean preferences*, which I will share with you." Here they are, in his own words:

My selective eating habits have been challenged on occasion by an adoring wife. In her loving yet devious manner, she confesses that she has laced my chicken soup with broccoli, hiding it beneath the nuggets of noodles. It is not just that I don't like broccoli; it is more that I see that veggie in a class with the kind of stuff you would only eat on a dare. It is a troubling food in more ways than one. It's difficult to chew it, to smell it, and to swallow it. It doesn't even let you bury it on your plate when it's served at someone's home and it would be rude to just ignore it.

The woman I am married to is a gourmet cook. She has a determined dedication to my well-being. When she has decided to serve me florets of broccoli hidden in pasta or slipped into my soup, she will distract me with an adoring look and an innocent smile.

I am not a picky eater. I just hate broccoli—almost as much as I am repelled by any kind of cheese, yogurt, spice, and most other vegetables.

Wow, it's a good thing he's not picky! If he was, I can't imagine what else he would refuse to eat. When I have him over for dinner, I have to remember that he won't eat anything creamy (except rice pudding), and he won't eat anything with whole grain, because he says it tastes like "bird seed." And then I take great pleasure in tricking him into eating lots of the healthy foods he says he won't touch.

THE MALE PSYCHE AROUND FOOD

"You don't marry someone you can live with; you marry the person who you cannot live without."

—*Author unknown*

To any woman who has been in a relationship for more than two weeks, it is clear how men approach food. For the most part, they're like lions at a kill. Just watch a bunch of men trying to close a business deal and you'll see the same attitude: "I'm going to get my share, even if I have to rip it out of someone else's jaws." Of course, all that goes on beneath the surface. They're civilized, after all, and know how to present themselves. But the drive is there nonetheless.

Nothing is dainty about a man's approach to food. Food is fuel. Dinner is the same as taking the car to the gas station to fill it up. No one wants to walk around with an empty tank. It has to taste good, yes, but more than anything, it has to leave them feeling full.

A man often says he wants something he can "sink his teeth into." There is a distinctly masculine quality to chewing or gnawing on foods like meat, which accounts for the fact that when you ask most men where they want to go for dinner, they answer, "a steak house." They also like to crunch, as on potato chips or hard pretzels. Alfalfa sprouts and yogurt just won't do.

A woman, on the other hand, might have just this for lunch. She tends to choose more delicate foods, which men typically call "chick foods." That is: the proverbial quiche, salads, broccoli florets, and cottage cheese. When a man goes on a diet, he chooses protein; when a woman goes on a diet, she chooses vegetables. I'm not necessarily saying that the woman adores alfalfa sprouts, but she will make the sacrifice for the goal of staying healthy and thin.

It has been suggested that one of the reasons men so often choose "manly" foods is that the masculine attributes of strength and invincibility go along with them. When you hear a man say, "I'm a meat-and-potatoes kind of guy," we all know what that means. Unfortunately, oftentimes men's sense of invincibility makes them reluctant to go see a doctor when something is clearly wrong. Statistics show that men avoid doctor visits far more than women; they are, in fact, 40 percent less likely than women to see their doctors. Perhaps they're afraid to acknowledge that a doctor's visit will make them feel weak or out of control. Some of them avoid going because they don't want to hear the truth; it might require them to change their lifestyle or face their own mortality.

If men won't drag themselves in when they're sick, they certainly won't seek medical advice for preventative wellness. Women are the ones who drag them in for routine screening tests and annual "well" visits. For many men, if they visit the doctor at all, it is as a last-resort answer to a major health emergency. In other words, when they're actually in the midst of a heart attack, they'll submit to riding in an ambulance.

"It's no longer a question of staying healthy. It's a question of finding a sickness you like."

—*Jackie Mason*

Men's reluctance to care for themselves is a compelling reason why women are smart to be vigilant about their guys' diets. If the men won't indulge in a little preventive care on their own by going in for regular medical check-ups, then we have to provide our own preventive care in the form of a healthy diet. There is no question that having women in their lives is good for their health. Research shows that married men are healthier and eat more vegetables than their bachelor buddies. According to a Harvard School of Public Health study of nearly 30,000 men, vegetable intake declined by more than three servings per week in men whose spouses had died, and nearly two servings per week for men who were divorced. Divorced men also consumed more alcohol and were more likely to eat fried foods. My grandmother always told me that "The way to a man's heart is through his stomach." I would add to that, "The way to a man's *health* is through his woman."

WHAT'S A GIRL TO DO?

I don't mean to sound like I'm picking on men. The fact is that none of us eat enough fruits and vegetables. The United States Department of Agriculture (USDA) recently upped their minimum recommended quota of fruits and vegetables from five to nine per day, giving us four more reasons to feel guilty. According to the Centers for Disease Control and Prevention (CDC), about 75 percent of Americans don't eat five *or* nine a day—but that figure climbs to 95 percent if it's limited to men. On average we Americans eat just one serving of whole grains each day, and almost half of Americans eat no whole grains at all.

What we *are* eating plenty of is simple carbs, saturated fat, sugar, and empty calories. It is an often-stated fact that our nation is overfed and undernourished, with obesity and illness rates rising daily. Unfortunately, our men are doing more than their share to keep this trend going. They eat too much of the wrong foods, and they don't engage in enough activity. The result? "Diseases of lifestyle," like Type 2 diabetes, heart disease, high blood pressure, and some forms of cancer. According to the CDC, the average American man lives 5.3 fewer years than the average woman. In 2003, male life expectancy was 74.8 years, while female life expectancy was 80.1 years.

"The word 'aerobics' came about when the gym instructors got together and said, 'If we're going to charge $10 an hour, we can't call it jumping up and down.'"

—Rita Rudner

A disease of lifestyle means an illness that isn't a random act of the universe, but is caused by one's own behavior. None of us wants our men to become ill from something that could have been prevented, but what can we do? Give up and call it a day? Is there no alternative to giving up and accepting an early death for the man we love? One woman I interviewed for this book told me it was hard enough to police her own habits. She told me, "I've given up spending energy on worrying about what my husband eats because I'm not his mother, nor do I want to be. I figure he's a grown-up and has to take responsibility for himself, for better or worse. So if he's going to go on eating badly, the most important thing I can do is to make sure he's got a really good life insurance policy!"

Sorry, but I don't consider this a viable solution. The issue of our men's health is too important to simply give up. As with my kids, I knew there had to be a smarter approach to getting my guy to eat the right foods. After nagging didn't work, I decided to try on my husband the same Sneaky Chef approach that worked so well on my kids. At least I could slip more nutrient-rich beans, whole grains, vegetables, and fruits into his favorite dishes to help mitigate any damage he was doing when I wasn't preparing his meals.

SNEAKY DOES IT

I turned my eye from kid meals toward men's macho meals. The men I interviewed for this book gave me tons of ideas for the kind of foods that guys traditionally like to sink their teeth into: meatloaf, mashed potatoes, burgers, chips and dips, chili, pies, dressings, and hash. Many of the "sneaky" superfoods that were used for the kids' book—like cauliflower, zucchini, spinach, broccoli, peas, carrots, yams, blueberries, white beans, wheat germ, and oats—are just as applicable when confronting men's health issues, and I've used them here as often as possible. But there are also some health concerns that are specific to adults, so I've added antioxidant-rich cocoa, green tea, and pomegranate, omega-3-rich sardines and walnuts, lycopene-laden tomatoes, and anti-inflammatory foods like cherry, ginger, garlic, and cinnamon.

The "decoy" foods—the ones that distract the eye and tongue away from healthy additions—had to be tweaked for men's palates as well. Based on the interviews, I chose spices like cayenne, jalapeño, or chipotle peppers, smoky turkey bacon bits, and dark chocolate.

"Vegetables are a must on a diet. I suggest carrot cake, zucchini bread, and pumpkin pie."

—*Jim Davis*

At first I questioned the need for visual methods to make men's food have a delicious image. After all, this book was for *adults*. Did it really matter what a dish looked like? But in my research I found, overwhelmingly, that men are primarily visual creatures. Whether it's their woman, their car, or their house, men go for the visual first. Their tendency is to be attracted to the package.

Hiding broccoli in the meatballs, or spinach in the chili, is just like putting on lipstick and high heels. We're simply dressing the food up to make it visually appealing to a man. Once he "gets to know" the disguised vegetable, he may be more willing to overlook her flaws and accept her for the substance she delivers.

THE GOOD NEWS

Using the recipes in this book will definitely help you win the battle for your man's health. The good news is that it is not an entirely uphill struggle to appeal to your man's own instincts and intelligence. A few pages back, I may have made the mild suggestion that men have some similarities to children when it comes to eating, but there is one huge difference: *Men can see the big picture.* This is a heavy-duty tool that you can use to your advantage, because they know that eating right is connected to long-term health. Aging Baby Boomers are especially aware of this, certainly more than their parents were, and many of them are now hitting their first health crises (nothing challenges the comfort of the status quo like a little heart attack). And if it hasn't happened to them, they are witnessing a friend or a colleague go through some sort of medical emergency. I have seen more than one male friend ex-

perience an extreme wake-up call when realizing that they are older than their own fathers were when they died. That is an extremely sobering thought!

In spite of the fear factor, it's still hard to change. This is, after all, the "me generation." We want to have our cake and eat it, too. But taste *rules*—and that's all there is to it. Men certainly don't want to give up their favorite foods, and if they do give them up for a brief period, they usually rebound all the way to the other extreme and eat even more decadent foods than they did before. But they also don't mind if their favorite foods are somehow doctored-up to make them healthier, as long as they magically retain the same great taste. I interviewed a number of firemen in the course of researching this book, and they all said that if I could make their meatloaf, mashed potatoes, and chili somehow healthier, while retaining the great taste and satisfying texture, they would be thrilled.

Another difference between men and children is that most men will eat *some* vegetables; it's just that they'll consume them along with the other crap they love. They tend to cover up the veggies with tons of added butter, cream, or cheese. The trick to cooking healthier foods, I found, was going to be in lowering the fat. I made that one of the main goals of this book.

AVOIDING THE YO-YO SYNDROME

"Be enthusiastic. Remember the placebo effect . . . 30 percent of medicine is show biz."

—Ronald Spark

If we want any sort of change to work, we have to familiarize ourselves with a little thing called "the rubber band effect." The idea is that a person is already formed in a distinct way and will bounce back to that form whenever there is change. If your man has been a couch potato for twenty years, he might enter a period of activity that he will keep up for a while. But eventually, his own nature will overtake him, and he will return to his "natural state" as a couch potato sooner or later.

We see this all the time when we try to change long-held habits. A major health crisis will scare us to death, and out of sheer terror, we will vow to change. We'll make a valiant effort, convincing ourselves and everyone around us that we are a new person and that our former sins are a thing of the past. The new and virtuous self emerges like Venus on a half shell. We give up smoking and drinking, eat a low-fat diet, work out every day, go to bed early; we do everything we've been told is good for us. From zero to sixty in two seconds flat, we throw ourselves into an immediate and extreme reaction and hope that somehow we'll be able to keep it up. And for a period of time, we actually do. After the initial recovery, however, we begin to feel a little better. Here and there, we begin to slip and stop doing all the things that require discipline. "I don't want to jog two miles this morning. I've done it all week. It won't hurt if I skip today." "I can afford this piece of chocolate cake for lunch. I've eaten six salads this week already. Just this once."

And that's how it starts. Whenever you hear yourself saying "just this once," you know you're in trouble. Soon you are saying "just this once" several times a day. And then you give up completely and just do what you want.

The Sneaky Chef knows that men cannot keep up any kind of drastic change forever. Sooner or later the rubber band effect will come into play and they'll start looping back into their former selves. When the pendulum swings to an extreme, it is bound to swing back with a vengeance. Men cannot sustain a new lifestyle if they are gritting their teeth the entire time. Once a health alert passes and they are feeling better, they lose the drive to overcome the sometimes-intense resistance and then become complacent. That's when they fall right back into the old habits. Usually this takes place within three to six months, depending on the nature of the initial crisis. They are back to eating what they want, accepting the illusion of invincibility, because their bodies aren't sending off crisis messages for the moment.

For the *Sneaky Chef*, the good news is that men don't necessarily have to keep up that level of vigilance. These recipes are as close as men will ever get to finding a magic pill for mitigating the evils of their poor lifestyle choices. If they can rely on a "pill" to fight the problem, it is far preferable to a lifestyle change. I have seen men eat the Sneaky Chef food and brag, "I can eat what I want and the magic pill will fight the high cholesterol, blood pressure, or diabetes." This feeds right back into their illusion of invincibility and their notion that they won't have to be inconvenienced by change.

It might sound a little wrong-headed to go along with the illusion of magic pills, but if it works, why fight it? The fact is that combatting the rubber band effect is so difficult that it's almost impossible (unless your guy is especially disciplined!). The reason is that we simply can't live at a heightened alert all the time. Understanding this will make it easier to forgive our men and ourselves for "being weak." Even if we have a severe heart condition, we can't be terrified of it forever. Eventually we will push it to the back of our minds.

The psyche needs to live in a relaxed

state. We always return to our favorite unhealthy comfort foods, eager to embrace the illusion that everything's fine. The Sneaky Chef recognizes this fact and changes the unhealthy food into something with nutritional substance. No more dieting. No more rebounding. Men can continue to eat their manly meals, knowing that the magic bullets will keep them healthy.

WOMEN ARE THE HEALTH MANAGERS OF THE FAMILY

"Man does not live by words alone, despite the fact that sometimes he has to eat them."

—Adlai Stevenson

You might wonder why I'm addressing this whole book to women. Early in the process of writing this book, someone accused me of being sexist for just that reason. It was a man, and he thought I should direct the book to either spouse who wants to cook healthier for the other. Why would I assume that the wife is cooking for the man or that creating a healthy diet falls only on her shoulders?

How I wish he were right. But traditionally, and still today, women are usually the caregivers of the family. Women worry more about their husband's health than the other way around. They usually take a leadership role in the healthcare management and decisions for the family, and in most cases, women do the menu planning and meal preparation for their children and husbands. Two-thirds of the women polled in recent studies said they were the ones who prepared the weekday meals (although younger men are about twice as likely to do the cooking as men who are older than forty-five). According to the *New York Times*, women still do 80 percent of the food-related work at home.

According to David Satcher, M.D., Ph.D., former U.S. surgeon general, and the interim president of Morehouse School of Medicine, "Women are key to making inroads into the health of our men. It's women who get men to the doctor, convince them to follow health-care providers' recommendations, and make diet and lifestyle changes for the entire family."

We know that women are more likely to read food labels, follow the latest health news, and carefully choose foods according to their nutrient content. According to consumer surveys, women are three times more likely than men to choose fruits, vegetables, and/or salads as their favorite foods.

When my male friend challenged me, "Why are you just addressing women? Perhaps some men will do the cooking for their wives or girlfriends," I admitted that some men really do like to cook—but I still couldn't imagine any of them taking the care and time to enhance our favorite dishes with carefully thought-out ingredients they know will contribute to our well-being. Okay, there may be such a man out there, but I haven't met him yet. So if you happen to be the lucky woman who knows one, hang on to him and pass him a copy of this book!

TO TELL OR NOT TO TELL

"Health nuts are going to feel stupid someday, lying in hospitals dying of nothing."

—*Redd Foxx*

Though I don't want to encourage dishonesty or deceit in a marriage (in spite of the playful subtitle of this book!), the results of revelation can be counterproductive. Just like kids, when men know they are eating something their minds tell them they don't like, they may stop eating it—even if they genuinely enjoy it.

Of course, it's up to each individual Sneaky Chef to decide whether to let her man in on her kitchen secret. You know your man; I don't. I can only speak from my experience with my own husband. Overall, Rick is fine with the fact that I am taking the time and initiative to upgrade the nutritional value of his meals. He likes this. Rather than serve him what he considers "plain, boring vegetables," I'm adding them to his favorite dishes, many of which he feels are decadent foods. Now he can enjoy these macho foods with less guilt. But like any good chef, I don't reveal *all* my secrets. There are just some ingredients I cannot confess to sneaking (for instance, his dreaded sardines). There are, however, plenty of other healthy ingredients that he isn't passionately against, and I can happily tell him that he just ate them and didn't notice.

You might just test the waters on whether to tell your man the secrets of your recipes. Try it once. See the reaction. If he's furious and threatens never to eat your cooking again, then don't continue telling! If, on the other hand, he's enlightened and becomes a convert because this previously loathsome substance is no longer objectionable (or even detectable), then that's great.

But whatever you do, don't gloat. Don't do a "gotcha!" so that it looks like you've triumphed over him. The idea is to elicit his cooperation, not to win a battle. The ultimate goal is to get our guys to do better on their own. If you can sneak good stuff into his meals and prove to him that it can be delicious, then he might be more inclined to make healthier food choices when you're not around. By interrupting their conditioned responses and breaking their preconceived notions, the ultimate result of the Sneaky Chef tactic could be that men do more for themselves.

Healthy Food Really Works

This section is meant to support you in your quest for your guy's cooperation in adopting a healthier diet; it illustrates what works and why. There are so many diseases that are related directly to lifestyle: heart disease, high cholesterol, high blood pressure, diabetes, stroke, obesity, atherosclerosis, certain cancers (like colon and prostate), and diseases associated with smoking and alcohol and drug abuse. The fact is, if you change your diet, you change your health. Here are the main guidelines that will help you do just that, which I discovered as I conducted research for enhancing the recipes in this book.

- **Increase antioxidants.** They reduce the risk of coronary heart disease, diabetes, and certain cancers by fighting disease-causing substances in the body known as "free-radicals." According to the Centers for Disease Control and Prevention (CDC), cancer is the second leading cause of death for men, with lung, prostate, and colorectal cancers being the most common. Examples of antioxidants include beta-carotene, lycopene, vitamins C, E, and A, and other substances. They are abundant in fruits and vegetables, as well as in other foods including nuts and grains.

- **Increase phytochemicals.** These ward off age-related diseases, heart disease, and cancer, and keep your brain sharp—which is of particular necessity to aging Baby Boomers who don't want to be forced to retire early because they're going senile. You'll find them in colorful fruits and vegetables.

- **Increase "good" fats.** Omega-3 fatty acids and other healthy fats found in nuts, olives, avocado, and fish like sardines and salmon, help to lower bad cholesterol and triglycerides, reduce blood pressure, and diminish the risk of sudden cardiac death. They also improve physical and mental health by reducing inflammation in the body, which has been linked with heart disease, diabetes, arthritis, cancer, and dementia. They also fight depression and help improve moods.

- **Increase fiber.** Fiber promotes good bowel and digestive functioning and wards off certain cancers—in particular, colorectal cancer. High-fiber foods (like beans, whole grains, fruits, and vegetables) promote cardiovascular health, improve glucose tolerance (by reducing the rapid rise in blood sugar that occurs after eating carbohydrates), and help to prevent or manage diabetes.

NEGATIVE VERSUS POSITIVE

During so much of the past couple of decades, the focus has been on what to eliminate from our diets to achieve weight loss or better health. In the eighties, fat was the enemy (eat the bun, not the burger); in the nineties, it was carbs (eat the burger, not the bun). Now it's both! While there may be merit in these philosophies, I'd rather talk about what to *add* to our diets to achieve better health, not tell you another food group to avoid.

This book focuses more on positive nutrition, specifically what foods to include in your diet to prevent or combat the illnesses most likely to affect men today. That is not to say the recipes in this book are full of fat and sugar; I have secretly reduced these detrimental ingredients in every possible way. But I was far more interested in adding the superfoods that will reduce bad cholesterol, sugar, and blood pressure levels. I wanted to concentrate on ingredients that decrease the risk of cancer and help to prevent heart disease, type-2 diabetes, obesity,

and stroke. For example, one of my techniques is to cut the use of mayonnaise in chicken or tuna salad by using white bean puree. Yes, there is still some light mayonnaise in the sandwich, but I have eliminated a lot of saturated fat, and I've added fiber and tons of nutrients.

Every recipe makes use of the concept of "food as medicine." It hides ingredients that will prolong your man's life so the two of you can grow old vibrantly together—without depriving yourselves of the good life along the way.

Health and the Happy Home

"Men and women belong to different species, and communication between them is a science still in its infancy."

—Bill Cosby

As I made clear in the first chapter, I have no doubt that women are good for men's health. But how much do we want to belabor the point that men are lucky to have us and should listen to what we have to say?

I know (from experience!) that the worst time to tell your husband you're right is when you actually *are* right! The more right you are, the more overbearing it may feel to be on the receiving end of your rightness. It's easy to look disparagingly at your husband as he starts in on his second corn dog at a Fourth of July picnic. When you say, "Honey, are you sure you need a second one?" what you're really telling him is that he has a problem and that you are there to save the day by solving it for him. Think about how we feel when men do that to us. Here's an example of how that happens: we have an issue that's been bothering us, and we just want to talk it through. We only manage to get the first three lines out (if we're lucky) when he stops us and starts firing advice like bullets from a Glock automatic. He doesn't want to waste time listening; he just wants to fix the problem and move on. In no time at all, it begins to sound suspiciously like a lecture. His voice drones on and we stop listening.

"Nagging is the repetition of unpalatable truths."

—Edith Summerskill

The only thing worse than a lecture is outright nagging, which ups the ante by adding a little more aggression. We end up saying things that would make us cringe if it was played back to us on a tape recorder. "How can you do this to me? You're going to die of a heart attack and leave me a widow!" "Are you really gonna do this to your kids—make them into orphans?" "If you don't care about yourself, at least care about your family. Don't you want to live long enough to walk your daughter down the aisle?" "All you want to eat is potato chips and beer. You're worse than a caveman." Does any of this sound familiar?

Believe me, I can nag with the best of them. It is often the result of pure exasperation over my husband's refusal to change his lifestyle. No matter how many times I tell myself that it's counterproductive, in moments of blindness I fall into the trap anyway. I throw up my hands in frustration and my mouth opens all by itself. And then, there it is: "You're not gonna put that in your mouth, are you?"

I suspect that the real reason for this conduct is pure fear. I want to control his behavior so I can control how long he lives. It's naïve to think I can control either, but fear isn't rational. Neither is love. The truth is I adore Rick and I want him to be around for a long time. But the surest way to induce the very response that I'm trying to eradicate is to nag him about it.

"The way you cut your meat reflects the way you live."

—*Confucius*

Let's go down the list and articulate just how the dynamic of your relationship is affected when you approach his unhealthy eating habits in the usual, complaining way.

1. **Suggest to him that he's doing something wrong, and he'll react defensively. You create a particular mood with these kinds of remarks, and it's not receptive and open. Pointing out his bad habits sets up an adversarial relationship in** which you are the authoritarian and he thinks he has to be defiant.

2. **He will feel criticized and resent you for it, even if you're right—especially if you're right. How would you feel if your guy made a face at you and said you could afford to lose a few pounds? Even if you went ahead and lost the weight, you'd carry the resentment with you.**

3. **It sounds like you're blaming him, and we all know what happens to a conversation when it turns to finger pointing. You've stopped listening to one another. Your position is that you are right and he's wrong. You've turned the discussion into a battle that he has to fight. To keep his dignity, he cannot afford to lose. Even if he does reach a point where he agrees with you, he can't admit it because it means giving up ground and possibly losing the battle.**

4. **If this subject has been a constant point of contention in your relationship, then it's quite possible that the fatigue factor is settling in. If you say one word, or even glance at him, when he's putting food in his mouth, it triggers a defensive shut down in him. You can't discuss**

alternative food choices because it is now a closed subject.

5. You trigger a power struggle. On the surface, the argument seems to be about food, but soon it's about something else, and neither one of you knows what it is. You're really engaged in a power struggle that is devouring your relationship. So far, neither of you has ever won this struggle definitively, so what makes you think you will this time? When two people are vying for power, neither one is listening or receptive, even if they're pretending to be for the sake of appearances. Each person is just trying to get the other side to agree with him. Women are seduced by the idea of "making their case." We ante up all the reasons why the guy should do things our way. We believe that if we make the case well enough, then he'll finally give in and let us solve his little problem about eating. Good luck!

6. We approach our man with our usual method of nagging, or with a reasonable lecture about food, and think we're on sure footing. The problem is that we aren't speaking his language. Men speak the language of action. Action is what they respond to and respect. They are a lot more willing to go along with you if you spring into action than if you try to talk them into something.

This final point is precisely why the Sneaky Chef method works. If you serve him a steaming casserole topped with bubbly, melted cheese with broccoli hidden inside, he will happily eat it. If instead you lecture him about the importance of eating broccoli, he will resist. In his head, he will think of nothing but unsatisfying green stalks that will leave him feeling deprived.

The real secret behind the Sneaky Chef method is that you can finally stop trying to "fix him." You can stop the fighting and the frustration and the resentment, and instead create a loving atmosphere in the home. The irony of fighting over food is that the real motivation behind your nagging is not aggression at all. It isn't the need for power or the need to be right—it's love. So instead of trying to get him to do something he doesn't want to do, look to see what needs he is trying to fulfill and then help him to do so. Most likely, he wants something very simple from his meals: satisfying, filling, and good-tasting foods. With the Sneaky Chef method, you communicate in a way that he understands: action.

"A man never tells you anything until you contradict him."

—*George Bernard Shaw*

It's likely that you already see the folly in nagging and arguing to get your man off of steak and potatoes and onto salads and steamed vegetables—and yet it's hard to break the habit. But try taking personal responsibility for introducing the change in a way that doesn't cause him to react negatively, and you will be sold on my method. It will transform the whole emotional tenor of your relationship, at least as far as food is concerned. As conflicts die down, so too will stress, and reducing stress will *really* help him live longer. After all, what relationship is more central to

his life than the one he has with you? By reducing this sore spot you are bringing a new level of peace into your lives as a couple. Imagine a serene dinner hour when your mind is at rest because your guy is eating life-enhancing food that he is enjoying without feeling judged or deprived. Some say the reduced tension even leads to a better sex life, so not only will your man live longer, he will *want to* live longer!

"Life expectancy would grow by leaps and bounds if green vegetables smelled as good as bacon."

—*Tommy Smothers*

CHANGE IS HARD

Most of us have tried everything we can think of to help our men change their habits: cajoling, seducing, nagging, reasoning, arguing, and outright fighting. But we are dealing with *habits* here, and habits are stubborn little suckers. Once they're set, they just don't want to budge.

A college psychology teacher once gave a group of students an interesting homework assignment. They had to pick a personal habit, like picking teeth or clicking a ballpoint pen, and stop doing it for one month. When they reported on the assignment at the end of the month, most of them were shocked at the results. They found it almost impossible to change even the tiniest thing about themselves, and these were insignificant behaviors the students believed they could easily control if they just "put their minds to it." If it was that hard for them to change small habits, imagine how difficult it is to change a behavior that is as central to our lives as eating.

Once the mind is used to doing something in a particular way, it tends to harden like cement. The older we are, the harder it is for us to change. Yet, the older we are, the more it matters that we *do* change, especially where our eating habits are concerned. Nutrition really counts for aging bodies.

"Our bodies are our gardens. Our wills are our gardeners."

—*William Shakespeare*

When men are confronted with revamping their diet, they become overwhelmed. They're certain it means giving up the flavors they love, and they believe they'll have to live in a perpetual state of deprivation. These are only two of the false beliefs men harbor about changing their diets. According to the USDA, here are ten more of the most common misbeliefs:

1. **"It's too hard to eat nine helpings of fruit and vegetables a day."**

2. **"Fruits and vegetables take too much time to prepare. Meat is easier."**

3. **"'Nine a day' means eating them nine times a day."**

4. **"I won't like the taste of fruit or vegetables—ever."**

5. **"Eating fruits and vegetables is expensive."**

6. **"Eating fruits and vegetables is inconvenient."**

7. **"Fruits and vegetables aren't filling."**

8. **"It's too hard and time consuming to eat them."**

9. **"I already eat enough of them to keep healthy; it's not necessary to eat any more."**

10. **"Fruits and vegetables spoil too quickly, so buying them is a waste."**

In my experience, men often talk about vegetables as if they were outside their domain. Historically men have associated themselves with meat. In the hunter/gatherer societies of our distant ancestors, women gathered roots, berries, and vegetables, and men hunted. In the twenty-first century, when guys commandeer the grill, they feel like hunters standing over a fire, roasting the kill. But the meat that Neanderthal men brought home only *supplemented* the family diet. There wasn't a slab of meat on the bark/dinner plate every night, because humans just weren't fast enough to have continual success hunting down much faster animals. So if your guy complains that he's not built for a vegetarian diet, tell him that the most manly of men—cavemen—survived mostly on the roots, berries, nuts, fruits, and vegetables provided by their women.

Men use these myths to rationalize their way out of having to do something they don't want to do. So if men really don't like something that we both know is good for them, and they're willing to come up with at least ten myths to avoid the stuff, the only answer is to sneak it to them!

"Red meat is not bad for you. Now blue-green meat, that's bad for you."

—Tommy Smothers

"Shouldn't I ask him?"

One of the things that sometimes bothers women about using the Sneaky Chef tactic on the men in their lives is the idea of making a unilateral decision and carrying it out without the consent, or at least the participation, of their partner. With children, we don't mind this so much. We make choices for our kids all the time without asking for their input. But our partners are adults. As a general principle, partnered relationships are based on mutual cooperation and joint decision making. But I believe that when it comes to cheating in the kitchen, it is always acceptable to act in a loving way, without offering an explanation or seeking approval. Don't worry—if he doesn't like the dish you serve, you'll know about his disapproval soon enough!

By the same token, you need not be thanked or congratulated for your "sneakiness." Your guy's newfound health is reward enough. And if he loves the dinner you served, that's better still.

"Never go to bed mad.

Stay up and fight."

—*Phyllis Diller*

In the end, your husband's health is more important than your pride or your need for all things to be equal. It's easy to complain that "I shouldn't have to do this" or "he doesn't appreciate me." Perhaps there *is* truth to it, and in certain areas and at certain times, I would feel the need to validate those complaints and probably air them myself. But when my husband's life is at stake, when our life together is on the line, when his ability to be a father to our children is the issue—then those complaints pale in comparison.

ATTITUDE IS EVERYTHING

"The greatest discovery

of my generation

is that a human being

can alter his life

by altering his attitudes."

—*William James*

In this book, "sneaky" is meant in the most loving way. If you make being right your goal, then you won't accomplish the real goal of being healthy. Ultimately, it is my wish that all of our men start cooperating with our agenda and begin eating healthier on their own.

You may be the one who's done the research on the value of certain foods over others, and you may know a lot more about this than your man, but you cannot approach the subject with, "I'm the one who's right. You don't have a clue about this stuff." If that's how you really feel, practice restraint, and don't say it. In this case, a generous attitude will pay off in the end. It will make him want to cooperate rather than resist.

Another temptation that Sneaky Chefs sometimes give in to is what I call "Gotcha!" You know he hates cauliflower, and you manage to slip it into a casserole without him knowing it. After he finishes the last bite, you can't resist gloating that you "got him to eat it." If you gloat over the fact that you got him to eat a vegetable he hasn't touched in twenty years, you may have "won" that time, but in the future he won't trust you around his food.

The Sneaky Chef method is an experiment. It's hit-and-miss until you both can settle on meals that work. It means if he really detests a certain food and he doesn't want to eat it no matter what, abandon that food and try a nutritional substitute. We're not trying to sneak something into his meals out of spite or just to see what we can get away with.

"I am an optimist.

It does not seem too much

use being anything else."

—*Winston Churchill*

That brings me to another important point: don't aim for perfection. You'll just drive yourself crazy, and you'll tick him off. The Sneaky Chef doesn't expect perfection, only improvement. There is almost no way that your guy is going to make every meal of every day into a vegetarian health-o-rama. Initially, you have to be happy with the one hot meal a day you are probably cooking for him. When he goes off to work, he's probably still eating a Big Mac for lunch. But take comfort in two things. One, at least his dinner will be healthy. Two, many of the nutrient-dense meals that you're feeding him at dinner will mitigate the damage from lunch. For instance, the white beans you put in his crab cakes will

help escort the fat from the burger out of his body.

What I have found is that men begin to feel a whole lot better when they change the way they eat. After all, healthy food makes for healthy bodies, and good health just feels good! Who doesn't want that? Once the rewards of these changes reach the sensate level—that is, they're not just concepts in the brain—men don't have a lot of trouble gravitating toward the foods that make them feel light and invigorated. On their own, they start avoiding the foods that make them feel heavy and fatigued.

"The greatest wealth

is health."

—*Virgil*

Whatever you say to your partner on the subject of diet, the important thing is to be mindful of *how* you say it. Avoid sharp, critical, or demanding statements, because if you're looking for a receptive response, that is *not* the way to get it. A critical tone of voice makes a person shut down to you. I guarantee he's not going to think, "She might be showing no respect for me at all right now, but I guess I'll be a good guy and listen to her anyway." If the message is delivered with a bitter taste, the message will be refused. Pay particular attention to off-handed comments, because they cause damage. Be careful of remarks like, "Do you really want to end up like your father?" Remarks made in the form of questions need to be real questions rather than just jabs that make him feel like an idiot.

Since this is a book about food, my last word of advice may strike you as funny, but it might be a good idea not to talk about food at all. I say this because food isn't the real issue—health is. Talk to him about how he feels. Is he stressed out? Does he have low energy? Do his joints ache from carrying around too much extra weight? Asking him about himself as a way into a conversation about diet is a good way to make him receptive. Remember, it is always a bad idea to fight about food. The stress levels your man

will experience during the fight will be far more detrimental to his health than the fried chicken you're fighting over. If you can hold your tongue and take matters into your own hands by cheating in the kitchen, you will enhance your relationship with peace and love, and in some magical way, this will enrich the food you cook.

"To avoid sickness, eat less; to prolong life, worry less."

—*Chu Hui Weng*

The Lists

"There are four basic food groups: milk chocolate,

dark chocolate, white chocolate, and chocolate truffles."

—*Author Unknown*

The lists in this chapter are meant to arm you with the information you need to shop smart and eat well. You can post the a photocopy of the lists on the refrigerator (right next to your guy's fantasy baseball picks) so you know right where to find them. Once you've referred to your lists for a while, they will become second nature to you. You'll never forget anything again. As

you buy the "In" items in this chapter over and over, you'll be teaching yourself which brands are the best, distinguishing them from the products that are genetically altered or highly processed, with loads of trans-fats, salt, sugar, and additives. In other words, the lists let you shop fast and smart.

Everyone knows that to eat smart, you have to start with buying smart. As with everything in life, it helps if you do a little research before you set out with your checkbook. When you're strolling down the aisle of the grocery store, you have to choose wisely. You certainly have to make an extra effort to buy organic, or at least to buy products that have no trans-fats or pesticides, which is the minimum you can do to preserve your health. Nobody expects you to choose perfectly every time, of course, especially if you live in a region of the country where fresh and organic are hard to find. However, you can assess what's available to you and then make the best choices possible.

"I am not a glutton—I am

an explorer of food."

—*Erma Bombeck*

Before we cover the content of your list, I want to present a few tips about how to

shop. Following these simple suggestions will save you frustration, money, and time.

1. **Always shop with a list! The quickest way to waste time and money is to shop for food** without **a list. You'll buy at least eight things just because they're on sale, even if you already have a pantry full of them.**

2. **Find out when your store restocks fresh fruit and vegetables (usually it's once or twice a week) and arrange to shop on that day.**

3. **Read labels for important information, like levels of trans-fats, saturated fat per serving, salt, and sugar content.**

4. **Shop the perimeter of the store where healthier items like fresh produce are located; limit time on the interior aisles, where the processed food is shelved.**

5. **Buy in bulk only if you're sure you'll use it. It's not a bargain if it ends up in the garbage.**

6. **Have a pencil ready in the store so you can cross items items off your list and add new ones.**

7. **Bring your own bags. Do a little something for the environment.**

8. **If you know your store well, arrange the items on your list on an aisle-by-aisle basis. You'll be amazed how much time this saves.**

9. **Go through your recipes before you go to the store, and make your list based on them. I know this sounds obvious, but it's easy to forget.**

10. **Don't shop when you're hungry or thirsty. If you're hungry, your stomach will call out to you, "Buy, buy buy!" If you're thirsty, you'll rush and forget things.**

11. **Avoid shopping at convenience stores or small corner stores; they're far more expensive.**

12. **Stick to your list and avoid impulse buys. The foods you buy on impulse are likely to be bad for you.**

"Tell me what you eat, and I will tell you what you are."

—Anthelme Brillat-Savarin

List One

THE TWELVE MOST IMPORTANT FOODS TO BUY ORGANIC

Sometimes referred to as the "dirty dozen," the following fruits and vegetables have been found by the USDA Pesticide Data Program to be the *most* contaminated with pesticide residues. Therefore, they warrant buying organic whenever possible. You will notice that most items on the list below have either thin skin or no skins, which is the reason they are exposed to more pesticides, and ultimately the consumer ends up ingesting them. If you eat these foods on a regular basis, you are exposing yourself to more than twenty different pesticides per day. The produce is cataloged from the *most to least* contaminated.

Peaches

Strawberries

Apples

Spinach

Nectarines

Celery

Pears

Cherries

Potatoes

Bell peppers

Raspberries

Imported grapes

"It's bizarre that the produce manager is more important to my children's health than the pediatrician."

—Meryl Streep

List Two

THE TWELVE LEAST CONTAMINATED FOODS

One other way to reduce the impact of pesticides is by stocking up on the foods in this list, which represents the USDA's "least contaminated." You can further reduce the amount of pesticides by remembering to thoroughly peel (when it's appropriate) and wash fruits and vegetables. Both of these actions have been shown to remove detectable pesticide residues. If you buy conventional produce from this list and follow those steps, you are only exposed to about two types of pesticide per day. You'll notice that most of these items have thick skins (or natural casings) that you don't eat, such as corn husks, pineapple skins, avocado shells, pea pods, onion skins, and banana peels. That skin is what protects the flesh inside from sprayed pesticides. This list is presented from the *least to most* contaminated.

Sweet corn

Avocados

Pineapples

Cauliflower

Mangoes

Sweet peas

Asparagus

Onions

Broccoli

Bananas

Kiwis

Papayas

The "In" and "Out" List for Men

"No man in the world has more courage than the man who can stop after eating one peanut."

—*Channing Pollock*

I don't know when food became so gender-ized. Back when our ancestors ate boiled rabbit or roasted hog or mutton stew, were any dishes considered masculine or feminine? Maybe food was so hard to come by then that people couldn't afford to be so particular. Nowadays, hardly a month goes by when *Maxim* magazine doesn't run an article on the newest tailgate food craze, which is shorthand for "guy food." Many dishes are clearly earmarked for one sex or the other, and I suspect we'd better obey the hidden "rule makers." Here, then, is the official record of what you can and cannot eat if you are a man and you want to be seen as one!

IN

Anything barbecued (even a tennis shoe!)

Red meat

Potatoes (mashed, scalloped, French fried, whatever)

Bacon

Spicy food

Coffee

A good stiff drink

Crunchy chips

Tailgate food, which means anything eaten out of the back of the car in the parking lot at a football game

Couch potato food, which means anything on the coffee table that can be reached from the couch or reclining chair

Fish (if they caught it themselves)

Chocolate

Beer

Protein bars

Chips and salsa

Marinades

Chile peppers

Dips

Sandwiches

Deli meats

Steak sauce

Pickles

Nuts

Beef jerky

Protein shakes

Anything on the indoor grill

Hot sauce

Deli sandwiches

Bar foods

Pizza

Beans (but only for the after-meal
sound effects!)

"If the body be feeble,

the mind will not

be strong."

—*Thomas Jefferson*

OUT

Quiche

Salads

Alfalfa sprouts

Yogurt

"Chick food"

Anything green and stalky

Cottage cheese

Dainty sandwiches without crusts

Tofu

Light foods

Wine spritzers

Health food

Cauliflower

Broccoli

List Five
STAPLES TO BUY

Now that we've established which foods are essential to buy and which ones you'll want to avoid, we need a list of staples that will help you use the recipes in this book. The following lists include all the superfoods, with essential vitamins and minerals, that you are going to be sneaking into the recipes, plus the foods your guy really likes to eat.

Together, they form the Sneaky Chef's best combinations. These days, you should be able to find an organic version of many of the items mentioned here.

PRODUCE:

Baby spinach

Zucchini, fresh

Broccoli, fresh

Sweet potatoes (or yams)

Cauliflower, fresh

Garlic

Ginger

Onions

Fresh berries, in season

Bananas

Avocados

Potatoes, russet

Lemons

"A nickel will get you on the subway, but garlic will get you a seat."

—*Old New York proverb*

MEATS/FISH:

Beef, lean, ground

Turkey, lean, ground

Salmon filets, wild

Chicken breasts, skinless and boneless cutlets

Chicken breasts, skinless with bone

Chicken wings, buffalo

Pork tenderloin

Turkey bacon, ideally without nitrates

CEREALS/FLOUR:

Wheat germ, unsweetened

Oat bran

Rolled oats, old-fashioned (not quick-cooking)

Cereal, high fiber flakes

Flour, whole grain blend, ideally Eagle Mills All-Purpose Flour made with Ultragrain

Flour, whole wheat (stone ground)

Flour, white (unbleached)

Cornmeal, stone ground

Polenta, stone ground

RICE/PASTA:

Brown rice

Pasta, manicotti noodles, ideally whole wheat

Lasagna noodles, ideally whole wheat "no boil"

BREAD:

Bread, whole wheat

Tortillas, whole wheat, flour

Tortillas, corn

Bread crumbs, whole wheat

Pita bread, whole wheat, "pocketless"

CANNED GOODS:

Artichoke hearts, in water

Chipotle peppers in adobo sauce

Garbanzo beans ("chickpeas")

White beans ("butter beans," navy, or
    cannellini)

Refried beans, low-fat, vegetarian

Baked beans, vegetarian

Tomatoes, plum, whole

Salmon, wild

Sardines, in water, skinless and boneless

Tuna, in water (preferably "chunk light")

Tomato paste

Evaporated skim milk

Manwich® Sloppy Joe Sauce

JARS/BOTTLES:

Baby foods, ideally Beech-Nut® Stage 1
    or Stage 2, sweet potatoes, carrots,
    blueberry/apple, country garden
    vegetables, peas

Tomato juice, low-sodium

Mayonnaise, light

Mustard

Pomegranate juice, 100% pure

Salsa

Pasta sauce

Vinegar, cider

FROZEN FOODS:

Blueberries, frozen (preferably without
    added syrup or sweeteners)

Strawberries, frozen (preferably without
    added syrup or sweeteners)

Cherries, frozen, pitted (preferably
    without added syrup or sweeteners)

Green peas, sweet

Corn, yellow, off cob

NUTS/OILS:

Tahini (sesame paste)

Walnuts, unsalted

Almonds, blanched and slivered

Extra-virgin olive oil, cold pressed

Canola oil, cold pressed

Walnut oil

Almond oil

Cooking oil spray, ideally pure olive oil

TEA/COCOA/COFFEE:

Cocoa powder, unsweetened

Green tea

Coffee, instant granules

DESSERTS:

Dark chocolate

Chocolate chips, semisweet

Frozen yogurt, low-fat

"Food is an important part

of a balanced diet."

—Fran Lebowitz

DAIRY/EGGS:

Blue cheese

Yogurt, low-fat, plain

Cheese, low-fat, shredded

Ricotta cheese, low-fat

Tofu, firm block

Eggs (with added omega-3 fatty acids)

Egg Beaters, liquid, in carton

Parmesan cheese

SPICES:

Cinnamon

Garlic powder

Onion powder

Cumin

Ginger, ground

Cayenne pepper

Chili powder

Hot sauce, like Tabasco

Red pepper flakes

Jalapeño pepper slices

Salt, ideally Original Himalayan
   Crystal Salt

OTHER:

Chicken broth, boxed (no MSG; low-sodium)

Vegetable broth, boxed (no MSG;
   low-sodium)

Honey

Pure maple syrup

Pure vanilla extract

Baking powder, ideally non-aluminum

Baking soda

Powdered sugar

Brown sugar

Jam, no sugar added

Worcestershire sauce

Soy sauce, low-sodium

Popcorn, unpopped kernels (not microwave)

Parchment paper

TOOLS:

Mini food processor, 3-cup capacity,
   ideally, KitchenAid 3-Cup Chef's Chopper®

Mini Bundt (or a "donut") pan

Muffin cups

CHAPTER FOUR

The Sneaky Chef's Bag of Tricks

"Home cooking: where many a man thinks his wife is."

—Author unknown

In my first book, all the ideas in my bag of tricks were designed to fool children. Strangely enough, the same Sneaky Chef methods that work on children often also work on adults. Almost everyone likes the taste of smooth and creamy, for instance. Everyone likes crunchy. Everyone wants to eat a dish that is pleasing to the eyes. These common elements are the basis of some of the methods I use to make health food taste better than junk food. Other methods are designed either to add a healthy ingredient to a dish, like combining unrefined flour with refined, or to use a health-wise cooking technique, like steaming or boiling food instead of frying it.

The following is a full list of the methods that we will use throughout the book. I discovered them through years and years of testing. I assure you that these methods really do work. The first one, especially, we will use quite a bit.

Method One:

PUREE

Pureeing—meaning simply to pulverize food until it is silky in texture—is the most basic and important of all of the tools used by the Sneaky Chef, mainly because we are all naturally drawn to foods of this texture. Maybe it's because pureed food reminds us of the comforts of baby food, and we never really outgrow that. How else do you explain the continuing popularity of mashed potatoes, creamy soups, and guacamole? Not to mention flan, crème brûlée, mousse, and pudding.

For the Sneaky Chef, pureeing has an added bonus: Changing the appearance and consistency of a food makes it easier to hide it in another recipe. My aim has been to find the healthiest products I could puree and then to seek recipes they could be blended into seamlessly. There are many foods that our men won't go near in their virgin condition—broccoli, for instance—that seem perfectly edible once they're pureed and mixed in with other less-objectionable ingredients. Even if the men know the puree is hidden in the dish, it doesn't bother them anymore, because the texture has been transformed. Pureeing changes the objectionable traits that the food possesses in its natural form so that it becomes unrecognizable in any dish that it "fits" into. (More about that later—you can't add just any pureed food into any old dish.)

The great advantage of pureeing is that you have to add very little water, if any, to mash the food to the right consistency. Pureed food should be the consistency of mashed potatoes, not that of a smoothie. In other words, it's more solid than liquid. If there is too much liquid in the mixture, it will liquefy the whole recipe. A can of white beans, which I puree and use often in recipes, requires no more than one or two tablespoons of water to make a nice smooth bean puree. A head of steamed cauliflower requires almost no added water since the vegetable contains its own.

"There is one thing more exasperating than a wife who can cook and won't, and that's a wife who can't cook and will."

—Robert Frost

Methods of Pureeing

There are two main methods of pureeing.

1. A blender.

A blender not only purees, it liquefies, blends, frappes, chops, and shreds. It is best suited to working with liquids or already mushy solids rather than whole, chopped vegetables. It is also handy for chopping ice. In this book, I recommend it most often for smoothies, iced coffee drinks, and soups.

2. A food processor.

For most of the recipes in this book, I suggest using a small (approximately three-cup) food processor. The larger processors just don't work well unless you insert a large amount of food. If you don't own one now, you might consider purchasing one (most models are less than $40 and are small enough to keep handy on the counter). You will use it quite often for these dishes. You will find, as I have, that it is easier than any other task in the kitchen (such as chopping, for example).

FOOD ITEMS TO HAVE ON HAND FOR PUREEING:

Raw baby spinach

Carrots

Cauliflower

Berries

Onions

Tomatoes

Bread (crumbs)

Legumes (white beans, chickpeas)

Sweet potatoes

Zucchini

Bananas

Apples

Almonds

Walnuts

Cherries

Tofu

Peas

Broccoli

Health Benefits of Method One

Aside from the obvious benefit of getting your guy to eat spinach, broccoli, and other foods he wouldn't have touched otherwise, there is a secondary health advantage to pureeing: it presents food in a concentrated form, which means it is more nutrient dense. You'd have a hard time convincing most non-vegetarians to eat two whole cups of steamed cauliflower in a sitting. But if you puree the same amount, however, it comes

out to less than a cup, and that can be added to spaghetti sauce. In other words, you use a seemingly smaller amount for the same nutritional benefit.

You wouldn't think that it would be hard to get men to eat fresh fruit, since it's sweet and juicy, but very few consume the required three to five servings each day. But try pureeing those blueberries in the blender with strong coffee and ice and see how he likes it. That Sneak-a-Chino tastes like a high-fat frozen coffee shake, but it's actually a nutrient-dense powerhouse drink.

Method Two:
COMBINE REFINED AND UNREFINED

Unless you live under a rock on Mars, you've heard that whole grains are healthy, yet relatively few people choose to eat them instead of their white-bread cousin. Whole wheat pasta, for example, just doesn't seem to taste as good as white egg noodles. Pie crust, cake, muffins, or cereal—we seem to want it processed, with all the grain removed. I suppose that we all grew up with white, overly processed products, so now we can't shake the habit. And I don't suggest we do—at least not cold turkey. With Method Two, we make the change gradually, with an easy blend of white and whole wheat. You can wean your guy off pure white flour by gradually adding a little more whole wheat flour to his diet every week. Think of it as training his palate for the heavier texture. Eventually he'll forget that his bread, cake, and cookies ever tasted another way. You may never convert him entirely to stone ground or whole wheat or nine grain, but using a flour blend will allow your dish to retain a good deal of the usual texture and weight while still imparting substantial health benefits.

Even the giant food manufacturers know that the public's taste is changing. In the fifties, Wonder Bread sold itself as a wonder food, building kids' bodies in "eight different ways." Meanwhile, it was so soft and pliant that kids were rolling it between their fingers and making play dough out of it. They treated it like a toy, not food. Now we have a multitude of breads to choose from, and we know what healthy bread is supposed to taste and feel like. In the big supermarkets, there are just as many grain breads as there are white. Smart food companies are cleverly coming up with healthier bread that is silky and smooth (and even "white"). With this blend, we're doing something similar, trying to find the best of both worlds—a healthy bread that doesn't taste like it came from a rock quarry.

The method for this trick is simple. You create a blend of flours, combining the familiar light taste of refined white flour with the heavier, grainier texture of other grains, whole wheat, or both. In this book, many of the recipes call for a "flour blend," which means one-third white flour, one-third whole wheat, and one-third wheat germ. I found this to be the magic combination for retaining many of the properties of the original white flour without succumbing to it completely. Much as I would have liked to, I couldn't use all-brown whole grain flour because it was too dense and grainy. Being a Sneaky Chef means giving people what they think they want while making sure it contains what you know they need. Method Two does just that. Breads and desserts made with the flour blend seem like processed, store-bought brands, but they actually offer the same health benefits as whole grain products.

Health Benefits of Method Two

So many men today eat on the run. They grab a sandwich, take it back to their desk, and chow it down as they tap away at the computer. If you prepare your guy's sandwich, you can make his lunch worthwhile by ensuring that the bread on both sides of the salami is whole grain and the chocolate-chip cookies or the wedge of pie or cake is made with this Flour Blend. Gradually, he will accept it, and then he will like it. The old white flour products will begin to seem unsubstantial, so when he's not eating your cooking, when he's eating out at a restaurant or a bar and grill, he will still make the right choices. After all, men are always saying they want a hearty meal. What could be heartier than a thick slice of chewy, full-flavored brown bread?

Whole grain products add the fiber that keeps our digestive system working optimally; they contain important vitamins and minerals, as well as antioxidants and phytochemicals. Hearty grains reduce our exposure to chemically bleached, altered, and processed foods.

"Worries go down better with soup."

—*Jewish proverb*

Method Three
USE FOODS THAT HIDE WELL

If you read the word *sneak* in a crossword puzzle, what's the first thing you'd guess? *Hide.* That's the key to Method Three.

THE MOST COMMON "HIDING" FOODS YOU WILL FIND IN THIS BOOK:

Cauliflower

White beans

Blueberries

Zucchini

Plain yogurt

Raw baby spinach

Peas

Almonds

Walnuts

Low-fat ricotta cheese

Whole wheat flour

Broccoli

Avocado

Olive oil

Sardines

Sweet potatoes

Cherries

Oat bran

Wheat germ

Carrots

Tofu

Green tea

Some of these will surprise you. For instance, most people are shocked to learn that baby spinach has virtually no taste of its own. Consequently, it can be concealed in any number of recipes without anyone ever guessing; a real home run for you, because spinach happens to be one of nature's greatest gifts to the human body. (It's critical to use the *baby* leaves, however, since they have not yet developed that earthy, objectionable spinach taste of more mature leaves.)

If you follow these four basic principles, you'll be hiding like a pro in no time:

1. **Similar colors and textures work well together.**

2. **The healthy ingredient has to either enhance the overall original taste or add no taste of its own.**

3. **If you're going to hide an ingredient, it can't taint the final product. You cannot affect the look or the texture of the final product any more than you can the taste.**

4. **The added ingredient has to be good for you.**

The ingredient you add must meet three criteria. One is taste. It has to have no real taste of its own. In addition to baby spinach, tofu and white beans are excellent candidates. The second is texture. The ingredient cannot leave too much of a gritty, leafy, or unusual feel or an off-taste that will make it distinguishable from the main dish. (Having said that, I must add that certain highly desirable healthy ingredients can be used, even though they do leave some effects. There are ways to deal with them as long as the effects aren't too strong.) The tongue is an amazing appendage. It can taste the difference in a food it is used to, even if the change is minute. To be a successful Sneaky Chef, you have to be craftier than your husband's palate. That's why I've tested and retested the recipes in this book. They don't pass the Sneaky Chef test if they taste "funny" to your big eater.

"We are living in a world today where lemonade is made from artificial flavors and furniture polish is made from real lemons."

—*Alfred E. Newman*

The third criterion is visual similarity. If you want to get away with tricking the tongue, you have to make sure the eyes don't give the secret away. Therefore, leave out residual flecks of green, as well as lumpy, grainy, coarse, or harsh texture. Over the five-year period in which I learned to be devious, I realized that all my hidden ingredients had to pass not only the taste and texture tests, but also the visual test. If you miss the mark when you experiment with sneaking on your own, you'll find out about it soon enough, even if your husband's way of communicating his dislike for the change is that most of his meal is left on his plate. There are men who won't even try a dish they've been eating all their lives if it suddenly looks radically different—they just assume they won't like the new version.

It's very important for the added ingredient to be similar in color to the main dish. You don't want the added ingredient to change the color of the dish, because that would be an obvious tip-off that you've been "sneaky." For instance, if you want to hide something in mashed potatoes, you wouldn't use pureed broccoli, because it would turn the mashed potatoes green. You have to either match the color of the dish or add a color that simply doesn't change it. For the potatoes, you could add pureed white cauliflower and be just fine. In this book, the recipes steer clear of anything that makes a dish look unappetizing. In addition to being taste tested, every recipe in this book has also been color tested.

An intense change in the color isn't always a bad idea, though. Sometimes a new color works to your advantage. For example, if your team is playing the in the Super Bowl, the guys might love it if you bake a cake in team colors. Or you might deliberately intensify the color the dish is supposed to be; for instance, you could turn a red sauce electric red by adding more lycopene-laden tomato paste or hot chili powder.

If you decide to experiment yourself, cast your mind back to kindergarten. Remember the old color chart? The teacher told you that if you wanted to turn any color into a muddy brownish black, you just mix it with the color opposite on the chart. For instance, red plus green equals dirty brown. I may be enthusiastic about pureed spinach, but you'll never see me adding it to my bright red spaghetti sauce. It would end up looking like

the residue at the base of an oil well. Spinach works very well, however, in meat dishes and brownies. Yes, I said brownies. The rich brown is not altered by the green.

Health Benefits of Method Three

It's obvious, but I'll tell you anyway. The great benefit here is that you'll get your man to do the impossible. He will try out a vegetable he has never eaten before, or one he has sworn never to touch. As the great Houdini of the kitchen, you have made it disappear. If he can't tell the food is there with any of his senses, then he won't object to it being on the dinner plate. Out of sight, out of mind, into the mouth and the digestive system and forming a healthy body—all without an argument.

As I said in Chapter Two, the issue of how much you really want to trick your man is an issue only you can answer. I have done some pretty tricky tap dancing on this point myself. Where I draw the line is this: I don't mind being sneaky, but I don't want to be outright duplicitous. If my husband has stated explicitly that he does not want to eat a certain food, not intentionally and not unintentionally, then it feels wrong to go against his wishes. Though I look for wiggle room wherever I can find it, as long as I know it's good for him.

Method Four

SUBSTITUTE NUTRITIOUS LIQUID FOR WATER WHEN BOILING FOODS

This method works best when the food that is being boiled actually absorbs the liquid it is being cooked in, like rice, oatmeal, and pasta. Then you aren't losing nutrients to a liquid that will only be thrown away. The liquid you choose to replace the water has to both enhance the nutritional value of the dish and complement the taste. Just like your guy, I genuinely value taste—that's what makes this cookbook stand apart from standard health food cookbooks. You don't want to introduce

a flavor that makes his favorite dish taste foreign to him or that makes it less flavorful. For instance, you wouldn't simmer his oatmeal in spinach-laden Green Juice. I do suggest some combinations that seem unorthodox at first, though, so you might have to ask him to have an open mind once in a while. As I've said earlier, I've served real men all my recipes, and the ones that have made it in this book have been a huge success with the guys when they give them a try. I've had men drink my Minty Hot Cocoa with Green (Spinach) Juice and say, "I don't know what's in it, but it's great!"

"Condensed milk is wonderful. I don't see how they can get a cow to sit down on those little cans."

—*Fred Allen*

Here are some examples of liquids to use instead of water when cooking:

BOILED SUBSTANCE	NUTRITIOUS LIQUID
Rice	Chicken or veggie broth, green tea
Soups	Chicken or veggie broth, green tea
Oatmeal	Milk or blueberry juice
Hot cereal	Milk or blueberry juice
Sauces	Milk, veggie or chicken broth, green tea
Hot cocoa	Milk
Pancakes	Milk
Puddings	Milk
Dumplings	Chicken or veggie broth
Potatoes	Chicken or veggie broth
Pasta	Green tea; chicken or veggie broth
Marinades and onion soup	pomegranate juice

As you can see from the list above, I most often replace water with chicken or vegetable broth, blueberry or pomegranate juice, green tea, or milk. Of course, we all do need a certain amount of water in our diets, but it's best just to pour a glass and drink it.

The goal for keeping your guy healthy is to make him as vitamin and mineral rich as you can, so whenever you're tempted to prepare a dish the old way, using water, stop and think about it; you're missing a great opportunity to add vitamins and minerals into the dish. Liquids tend to either blend into the dish or evaporate entirely, leaving only the health benefit behind, so introducing extra nutrition in liquid form is the perfect sneaky way to do it—no lumpy foreign ingredient that he might notice and object to!

Health Benefits of Method Four

Water by itself doesn't add many nutrients to a dish, whereas nutritional substitutes do.

- Milk adds calcium, vitamin D, and protein.
- Blueberry or pomegranate juice adds phytochemicals and a day's worth of antioxidants and vitamin C.
- Green tea provides a significant dose of heart-protecting antioxidants and builds immunity.
- Vegetable broth provides potassium, calcium, and all of the essential minerals.
- Chicken or beef broth adds minerals and protein.

Method Five

COMBINE FOODS THAT ARE A SPECIFIC NUTRITIONAL COMPLEMENT FOR ONE ANOTHER

We inadvertently combine foods all the time, since most meals consist of more than one ingredient and most dinner plates have more than one item on them. The idea of Method Five is to combine foods intentionally, with benefits well beyond taste or variety.

What I am proposing here isn't new. Nutritionists have long known, for example, that protein from non-animal sources doesn't form a complete protein, since it lacks essential amino acids. If vegetarians want their bodies to absorb more protein from their diet, they consciously combine certain foods to maximize their potential. They start with a plant like a legume, which is a good but incomplete source of protein in itself; then they add another plant-based food, like whole grains, or a non-meat animal product, like milk or cheese, to form a more complete protein. Combining plant proteins makes up for the deficit of each individual food.

This process is known as "creating food complements." Doing so enables one ingredient to help the body fully utilize another nutrient. Magnesium, for instance, goes well with calcium, since it's known to increase the body's ability to absorb the calcium. Guys need calcium to maximize bone density. Hence, in several recipes I sneakily combine magnesium-rich white beans with calcium-rich cheese.

Method Five also allows the body to take in more iron. Everyone knows that women need iron, but men do, too. They need it to form myoglobin, a protein in their muscle cells. In bone marrow, it makes hemoglobin, the oxygen-carrying chemical inside all red blood cells. Iron deficiency is especially prevalent in pre-menopausal women; however, it can occur in men who have an inadequate diet or who just don't absorb iron from their food very well. When iron deficiency is mild, there aren't any real symptoms. When it is pronounced, a man will experience shortness of breath and be tired all the time. He'll want to start napping in the middle of the day, and he'll have a very hard time exercising.

The best sources of iron are red meat and certain fruits and vegetables, which you'll find plenty of in these recipes. It's also important that the iron consumed is actually absorbed by the body, and many recipes in this book were designed to increase absorption of iron. An example of this combination is the vitamin C-rich blueberries and iron-rich spinach in the Purple Puree, which I use in the Brawny Brownies, page 326, or Barbell Burgers, page 287.

Health Benefits of Method Five

For every recipe in this book, I have taken into consideration the ways in which specific foods complement one another and the benefit to be obtained from the grouping. The combination of ingredients in the recipes has been carefully thought out so the nutrients meld together to double or triple the benefits for the body. I have made sure that each recipe will not only be a "well-balanced meal," but also that it will appeal to your husband's appetites.

To keep my sneaky reputation, I had to disguise the combinations. So, for example, when your man sits down to a steaming bowl of sneaky Manhattan Clam Chowder, he's getting a complete and nutritionally-balanced meal, blissfully unaware that the vitamin C-rich tomatoes and cauliflower are helping him absorb the iron in the clams. This is one instance in which what he doesn't know will help—not harm—him!

The following is a fairly complete list of the food combinations you will find in this book, along with their health benefits:

Legumes + whole grains	
Whole grains + dairy	
Legumes + nuts	} Forms complete protein
Legumes + dairy	
Meat + tomatoes	
Blueberries + spinach	
Tomato sauce + beans	} Enhances absorption of iron
Potatoes + white beans	
Spinach + tomatoes	
Wheat germ + cheese or milk	
Ground almonds + milk	
Tofu + cheese	} Enhances absorption of calcium
Refried beans + corn tortillas/cheese	
Avocado + dairy	

Method Six

IDENTIFY FOODS MEN ARE LIKELY TO ENJOY STRAIGHT-UP

Sometimes men don't want a "dish" at all. They want simple finger food that they can eat with their hands. If you've ever gone to a lobster bake, you've had the chance to rediscover the joys of eating with your hands. It's primitive and sensual, and it brings a whole new aspect to dining. Perhaps that's why finger food is so appealing to guys when they're watching a game together on television. Yes, it's convenient, but they also enjoy grabbing a fistful of potato chips with their hands the way their distant ancestors would grab a drumstick off a dead ostrich and bite into it.

"After all the trouble you go to, you get about as much actual 'food' out of eating an artichoke as you would from licking thirty or forty postage stamps."

—Miss Piggy

Mindless snacking can really rack up the calories and fat, so do your guy a favor and put some healthy alternatives in front of him. Guys tend to take the path of least resistance. They like to keep it simple. Sometimes convenience will override other concerns and he'll eat whatever you put in front of him. He might impulsively grab a handful of crunchy roasted chickpeas instead of the usual high fat chips and be perfectly happy.

This whole book is geared toward making healthy foods as quick, convenient, and

tasty as the unhealthy ones. The following is a list of munchies that are unadorned whole foods:

- Peanuts, in shell (you have to work to get one out, especially in a dark bar with a beer, and they're not as salty as the ones in the little bags)
- Roasted chickpeas
- Snap peas (crunchy, sweet)
- Celery sticks with blue cheese dip (and a side of buffalo wings)
- Popcorn (for health, not all popcorn is created equal; get a good, natural brand with a little good oil, like olive oil—and caramel-coated popcorn doesn't count!)
- Frozen grapes (very refreshing!)
- Sunflower seeds, unsalted, in shell
- Pistachios, in shell, unsalted (not red-dyed)
- Edamame
- Whole roasted chestnuts, in shell
- Raw baby carrots, with dip (be sure to rinse them and pat them dry so they're not slimy)
- Olives (big meaty ones, but not too many)
- Granola, low-fat
- Shrimp cocktail, with hot sauce
- Chips (low-fat) and dips (hummus, guacamole, and salsa are best)

- Pretzels, whole grain, unsalted
- Artichokes, whole
- Sweet green peas, in shell
- Cherries
- Pomegranates, whole (he'll burn ten calories a second just digging the seeds out!)
- Corn-on-the-cob, grilled in a husk
- All berries

This is the least sneaky of all the methods in the book. In fact, nothing is actually hidden or disguised about serving foods in their natural, unadorned state. Try eating the food in front of him with a look of pure pleasure on your face, but don't say a word about it. Certainly don't nag him. In fact, the less you say about it, the better. If you start harping about the health benefits of edamame beans, they're no longer a snack—they're an issue.

For some strange reason, many of us have come to enjoy the taste of artificial flavors more than we do natural foods. Natural foods aren't overloaded with sugar and salt and cheese and so on; they're far more subtle. So the best way to get guys to eat finger food that hasn't been artificially messed with is to serve it alone and without competition. If the guys are playing poker, don't offer them a bowl of bite-sized fruit right next to a bowl of bite-sized candy. The candy will win, because the subtlety of natural flavors can't compete.

Health Benefits of Method Six

After World War II, TV dinners, canned food, frozen food, processed food, and take-out food exploded onto the scene, and as a country we practically abandoned eating whole foods like fruits, vegetables, beans, nuts, and grains. Prior to that, people ate vegetables, eggs, fruit, and milk that was produced within a ten-mile radius of their homes. Wives and mothers shopped every day at small local stores, and since everything was highly perishable, they only bought what could be eaten within a day or two.

But the 1950s brought progress, when mass quantities of foodstuffs were shipped to central locations in giant warehouses, which could then be distributed to different sections of the country. Suddenly, even if you lived in a house surrounded by farmland, the corn and beans grown there were likely to be shipped off to another state. The eating habits of Americans became homogenized. We started eating food that was pasteurized, loaded with preservatives, vacuum-packed, processed, canned, or frozen. The wonderful fresh products our great-grandparents used to enjoy were replaced by packaged foods that contain trans fats and artificial colors and flavors, not to mention copious amounts of sugar and salt.

The consequences of these developments are unfortunate. We Americans now eat more food and have less to show for it. The natural foods we've moved away from eating are low in calories and loaded with phytochemicals, vitamins, minerals, and fiber. They are more satisfying than processed foods, mostly because the fiber provides a feeling of satiation. With natural foods, there is no need to keep eating and eating because they help to stabilize blood-sugar levels so we don't feel hungry again an hour after a meal.

The health benefits of returning to the "old days" are so tremendous that there is a social movement afoot to do just that. The extraordinary growth of farmers' markets in cities and towns all across America attests to the fact that there is value to food from small farms that is grown with great care and without pesticides. We're beginning to rediscover the importance of "locally grown" produce and nature's untouched bounty, without interference from man. You'll become a part of this movement when you introduce fresh foods to the guy in your life. When he reaches for a snack, you can be sure he isn't getting empty calories.

"Our lives are not in the lap of the gods, but in the lap of our cooks."

—Lin Yutang

Method Seven

ALTER THE COOKING METHOD TO AVOID FRYING

When I'm in a restaurant and I see "crispy" fried chicken or "crackling" calamari on the menu, it may as well read "Heart Attack on a Plate." Diets featuring deep-fried foods place a strain on the body and seriously increase the risk of high cholesterol, heart disease, and obesity. I don't know why so many American restaurants haven't gotten the message that heart disease is on the rise. We're losing too many good men to heart attacks when they're in their fifties (which they say is the new forty, but for some it's the new sixty). Diets that are high in saturated fat raise bad cholesterol and dangerous triglycerides. Fried foods have a lot of saturated fat because the fat is cooked right into them.

Method Seven offers the fried food alternative we've been waiting for. I know that the American man loves his fried food, so I offer substitutes that mimic the crispy taste without the saturated fats. Instead of deep-frying, I bake foods at a high temperature with a mist of heart-healthy olive oil. It works especially well with "fried" chicken, calamari, onion rings, and French fries.

All fats are not created equal. When used in moderation, monounsaturated oil, like pure, extra-virgin olive oil, is one of the healthiest foods available. It helps keep "good" (HDL) cholesterol up and holds "bad" (LDL) cholesterol down. We just have to manage the amount of oils, even good oils, because they are dense in calories and fat and add to the waistline.

The mistake people make is to add oil when they first begin to cook, which makes the food dry out too fast. Instead, add the oil at the *end* of the cooking process so it doesn't dry out. You'll use much less oil and still retain all the flavor and benefits of cooking with fat. Adding the oil later also has a desirable visual effect; it leaves a golden luster and the texture of the food looks and feels crispy. I often recommend misting the dish with olive oil *after* you begin to oven-bake. The fine mist will give food a delicious-looking luminous sheen.

Some other techniques I suggest for reducing the amount of oil you use while cooking include:

- When you've finished cooking a food, blot off the excess oil with a paper towel. This is true even if you're pan-frying rather than deep-frying.
- Measure oil with a teaspoon instead of pouring it right out of the bottle.
- Baste oil onto your food with a pastry brush, which allows you to apply a small amount that evenly coats the food.
- Blast the dish with high heat under the broiler for a minute, to crisp-up the high fiber breading on many of my recipes.
- Use broth, instead of oil, to give a recipe the juiciness it needs to mimic fattier foods.

No matter how much guys should know better, they often go into denial when their mouth is watering for a nice fried steak. They think to themselves, "I'll be better tomorrow. Right now, I deserve that steak. I worked hard today. I really need the protein." Pointing out that they could get just as much protein from cottage cheese as they can from a juicy steak will not win you a "Woman of the Year Award." It's not that women don't also go into denial when they have a craving, but often a good look in the mirror will make them see the light of day. Your man might even be very good at curbing his desires in the short run, but in the long run he'll be tempted to give in to them. He can't hold out forever. That's why it's so important to make the dishes you give him look and taste like the food he's really hankering for.

"If I'd known I was going to live this long, I'd have taken better care of myself."

—*Eubie Blake (at age 100)*

Health Benefits of Method Seven

This is not a fat-free cookbook. In fact, I don't necessarily believe in fat-free cooking. I have known people who completely removed oil from their diets, and they paid a price with their health. Our bodies *need* good fats for building healthy skin, hair, and nails, and for assisting in the absorption of the foods we eat. Vegetable and bean dishes are full of fat-soluble vitamins and antioxidant phytochemicals, but the body needs oil in order to break them down. Monounsaturated and nut oils lower cholesterol levels, and some fatty products even impart essential omega-3 oils, which elevate moods and are good for the heart and brain. Therefore, our dietary goal shouldn't be *no* oil, but rather the correct amount of the right kind of oil. Don't think about helping your man control his weight by cutting oil out of his diet. Think about substituting the good oils in moderation.

You can't point the finger and criticize men for loving oily foods. Many scientists speculate that we are genetically predisposed to crave fat, the same way we are internally programmed to avoid the taste of poisons. It's the survival mechanism at work. Many scientists speculate that our craving for it is left over in our DNA from the old days, when our bodies craved it but we couldn't get it. The problem is that now oil is plentiful, and we don't get enough exercise to burn it off.

Of all the cooking methods available to you, deep-frying is the one to avoid whenever possible. The saturated and hydrogenated oils used for French fries and the giant bucket of chicken and the batter-coated vegetables—the usual fare at fast-food restaurants and sports arenas—are the worst culprits for clogging arteries. To bring home the point that these foods are the enemy, imagine a TV commercial in which the sheriff stares down a killer, who has the name "fried foods" tattooed across his hat.

Method Eight

Cut the Effects of Toxins or Fats by Diluting the Ingredients with Something Healthier

I know women who just have to stand back and scratch their heads when they watch their guy prepare a plate to eat while watching an afternoon game. Often this is his favorite food; he's been eating it for years. He probably has never stopped and asked himself if he even likes the food anymore; it's just a leftover favorite from childhood that he reaches for whenever he wants to eat something comforting and familiar. My husband's favorite snack when he was growing up is called *gribenes*. Essentially, it consists of crackling bits of fried chicken skin that are a byproduct of the process of rendering chicken fat. His grandmother used to make it for him, and he ate it "like popcorn!" If only his grandmother knew the damage she was doing!

The two most popular sandwiches for kids are peanut butter and jelly and tuna fish. While most guys outgrow PB&J, tuna often remains a mainstay. However, the ocean the tuna grow in is no longer as clean and toxin-free as it was when your guy was a youngster. These days, warnings aplenty advise parents to feed children tuna no more than once a week because of the high levels of mercury found in the fish. And if it isn't safe for kids, it can't be much better for adults. If your man has a fondness for tuna sandwiches, alter the sandwiches to be healthier by diluting the tuna with sardines, a great source of essential

omega-3 fish oil. A lot of people don't like sardines, but when a Sneaky Chef mixes them with tuna and light mayonnaise, very few notice the difference. Whether you let him in on your secret or not is up to you.

"What is patriotism but the love of the food one ate as a child?"

—*Lin Yutang*

Butter does not have any toxins per se, but for all the damage it does to his heart it may as well. Substituting an unsaturated fat like olive oil for some of the butter won't necessarily cut the calories in a dish (both have about the same amount of fat per tablespoon), but it will keep his arteries cleaner. So the next time your husband wants French toast or a grilled cheese sandwich, use a tiny dab of butter to give it some of the old flavor, use olive oil for the grilling.

Of course, you can't substitute oil for butter in every dish. Also, only use this method with like-substances that match closely in flavor, texture, and color.

Use your imagination for other ways to bulk up a dish with a healthier substance. Here are some other examples of Method Eight that you can implement in your cooking:

- Cut the fat out of creamy salad dressings by mixing in plain yogurt.
- Replace some of the butter in baked goods with a fruit or vegetable puree.
- Use pureed white beans in place of heavy cream in sauces. This technique also works for mayonnaise.
- Substitute evaporated skim milk for whole cream in creamy soups.
- Mix ground turkey or chicken into meatloaf, meatballs, and hamburgers to cut down on red meat.
- Use pureed white beans instead of cream in chowders.
- Cut the butter in cookies with a little healthy nut oil.
- Use half the usual amount of mayonnaise on sandwiches by mixing it with pureed white beans.
- Limit the cheese in pasta dishes by using

pureed tofu, which mimics cheese.

The secret behind getting away with sneaky tricks is to use just enough of the offending yet delicious ingredient to retain the original flavor. That's why the Sneaky Chef advocates using all healthy tricks in moderation. If the dish doesn't taste good, the trick doesn't work; if the taste, texture, and appearance are still familiar and the dish is satisfying overall, you can get away with it. I have found that as my eager eater grows accustomed to the flavor, I can add more and more of the good stuff to my recipes. In time, I've been able to wean my husband off of some toxic foods completely with barely a burp of protest.

Health Benefits of Method Eight

You are cutting down on toxic substances in your man's diet. Need I say more? You might even be ridding him of a habit with a hidden danger, like the mercury in tuna, which may have been impacting him without anyone being aware of it. Your man might wake up one morning, stretch, and say, "Boy do I feel good today!" He might feel good because he won the office football pool, but maybe it's because he hasn't eaten mercury for six months. Or perhaps it's because his heart doesn't have to work overtime to keep the blood pumping now that he's cut down on saturated fats. Or maybe the fifteen pounds he's lost since you eliminated half the butter and mayonnaise from his diet has finally gone to his head, lifted his spirit, and made him feel sexy again.

In a country that could be nicknamed "Junk Food Heaven," you can't avoid toxic foods entirely, even if your guy never eats a meal outside the house. However, you can mitigate the negative impact of bad foods by sneakily replacing them with healthier ingredients in the dishes you cook.

"If your dog is fat, you're not getting enough exercise."

—*Author unknown*

Method Nine
Cut Calories and Increase Volume with Low-Cal, Nutritious "Fillers"

Elizabeth Taylor was asked once how she managed to shed about eighty pounds in one year. She said she did it by always eating naked in front of a full-length mirror. Doing that took guts. If our men did that when they were snacking, they wouldn't unconsciously wolf down three packs of potato chips, chased by a beer and half a pizza. That's what's called mindless eating. The men probably started out mildly hungry, but they kept eating long past the point when their stomachs needed food. And what they ate had twice the calories they would have consumed if only they made a better choice when they first selected the snack. Snacking on peanuts, a dense caloric food, is healthy if your guy eats them in moderation. But if he eats a bucketful of oily, salted peanuts, however satisfying it may be, he will certainly bulk up—and not in a good way! If, on the other hand, he devours a bucket of homemade popcorn misted with olive oil, he will be just as satisfied at only a fraction of the calories.

With Method Nine, I add volume to food by using nutritious ingredients that add relatively few calories. I "beef up" the dish so my guy can eat to his heart's content without packing on weight. This is similar to Volumetrics, Barbara Rolls's system of weight management, which is a fairly new scientific approach to shedding unwanted pounds. It lets people eat as much as they want, but the beauty is that they don't want as much. Once they feel full (or, with some people, shortly after they feel full), they stop eating. In this weight-loss system, the meal simply contains more water and fiber. It makes good use of low-calorie, nutritious fillers to satisfy the diner. Some of the ways the recipes in this book use this technique are by adding:

- hidden vegetables to meat sauces.
- pureed fruit to homemade ice cream and smoothies.
- low-fat ricotta cheese to manicotti.

- pureed vegetables to macaroni and cheese.
- pureed vegetables to pasta sauce.
- pureed cauliflower to mashed potatoes.
- pureed white beans to light mayonnaise.
- diced tofu to egg salad.
- plain yogurt to cheesecake.
- pureed vegetables to guacamole.
- pureed beans and veggies to meat dishes.
- vegetables to meatballs or chili.

Mashed potatoes are my favorite dish for experimenting with this method. Though potatoes are high in antioxidants, when compared to leafy greens, they're relatively low in vitamins and minerals. By mixing in pureed cauliflower and zucchini, I can increase the amount of "potatoes" on the plate while adding almost zero extra calories. Your guy will look at the plate and he think he's getting a full serving. He'll eat it with a little bit of olive oil and plain yogurt in place of high-fat sour cream, and it will still taste like his favorite dish—but he actually will have consumed a full serving of cancer-fighting cauliflower as well!

Health Benefits of Method Nine

This method lets us consume far more nutrients and fewer calories while eating a greater volume. Its biggest virtue, then, is that it takes the sin out of overeating.

I tend to choose ingredients that are high in water, fiber, and nutrients, yet low in fat and sugar. These ingredients add mass to foods that are usually calorie-dense and high in sugar or fat. Water is a good additive because it really makes you feel full. Fiber is good because it lowers caloric density by providing bulk, while simultaneous benefitting the digestive tract.

The water and fiber content of fruits, vegetables, cooked cereals, and brown rice all make them a good fit with Method Nine. I limit the use of high-density foods like red meat, nuts, cheese, and chocolate because they have high fat and/or calories and sugar and are likely to land at the top of the food pyramid.

Method Ten
USE SLOWER-BURNING FOODS TO AVOID BLOOD SUGAR "SPIKE AND CRASH"

You often hear about men at the office going through withdrawal when they decide to kick the coffee habit. There are men who drink as many as ten cups a day in offices all over the country. Coffee is the second most valuable commodity in the world today; only oil is bigger. More than 50 percent of Americans drink coffee daily, which adds up to about 330 million cups per day! The sudden absence of caffeine gives men headaches and makes them feel unnaturally tired and groggy. But I wonder how much of that effect comes not from the lack of coffee, but from the sudden lack the two teaspoons of sugar they used to *put in* their coffee.

Sugar is known to cause a very quick rise in blood sugar levels. The spike is short-lived and is followed by a corresponding quick drop in blood-sugar level. Often it drops even lower than it was before the person ate, leading to a sense of tiredness and lethargy caused by energy depletion.

Men who stop drinking coffee also complain of being cranky, but that is also a sure sign of sugar withdrawal. People who are especially sensitive to a drop in sugar levels may feel shaky, irritable, and foggy. They often think they're hungry, even if they just ate. This effect is caused not just by white sugar, but by natural sugar, and even simple carbohydrates, which turn to sugars in the bloodstream. We all know that white bread and pasta are considered simple carbohydrates, but so are vegetables like white potatoes. Simple carbohydrates have an elevated number on the glycemic index (GI), which is a measurement of the effect a food has on one's blood sugar level. The higher the rating on the index, the more rapid the increase in blood sugar level.

The immediate goal of Method Ten is to slow the direct aftereffect of sugars. The long-term goal, however, is to stop the craving for simple carbs and their addictive quick-fix effect. It gets to be an unconscious habit; a guy reaches for a Danish in the morning because

he knows it will give him the rush he needs to get through the first meeting of the day. Perhaps the sweet roll will even take him through to the lunch hour, but by then he is starving because the sugar surge has dipped. Then he overeats, because he thinks he's hungry. Unfortunately, this begins a vicious cycle, where he has to keep grabbing the same kind of food just to keep up his energy. And of course, these foods are never the ones that are good for him.

"If God had intended us to follow recipes, he wouldn't have given us grandmothers."

—*Linda Henley*

You can end this habit by changing the "junk food" your guy reaches for when he's hungry. Grabbing a convenient Bonanza Crunch Muffin, page 160, will provide him with protein, whole grains, and enough fiber to maintain his energy levels throughout the morning and prevent the spike and crash that accompanies a high-sugar breakfast.

Instead of simple carbs, offer high-fiber "slow carbs." You have a number of choices here: whole grain breads and crackers, vegetables, beans, brown rice, oats, and whole grain pasta. All of these have a low GI rating. You're probably not going to be able to convert your guy overnight, so I recommend that you, the ultimate Sneaky Chef, *combine* low GI foods with spike-and-crash carbs to decrease the net effect. Pay attention to your guy's eating habits and figure out how you can substitute new and improved snatch-and-grab items. If he likes doughnuts, give him Legal Donuts, page 148, loaded with whole grains, fruit, and veggies. If he likes waffles, give him oat- and walnut-boosted Wiley Walnut Waffles, page 157. With these dishes, the combination of low-GI foods *with* high-GI foods lowers the GI value of the whole meal and produces a slower rise in blood sugar.

It's important that none of the "switches" is obvious. After all, the whole reason he's reaching for his favorite junk food in the first place is that he wants a cer-

tain taste, and he wants to feel satisfied when he's finished. If his palate is attracted to a heavy dessert and you give him a heavy slice of angelfood cake, he's going to push it aside to go after what he really wants.

You can't expect perfection, only improvement. He's going to eat something made with sugar and starch—that's just a given. But you can make sure there's some fiber and nutrition in his morning muffin, instead of just empty calories. And if your muffin really does its job, it will stabilize his blood sugar level so he won't crave another snack right afterward. He'll probably be clueless as to why your Blockbuster Blueberry Muffins, page 158, hit the spot. He can't (and shouldn't be able to) guess that they contain sneaky white bean puree and oat bran, with less than half the fat and sugar of regular muffins. The only one who knows these little secrets is you, and you're not telling.

Some of the best nutritional boosters you will find in this book are:

- oat bran in brownies, cookies, and muffins.
- pureed white beans and veggies in biscotti and muffins.

- tofu in cheesecake.
- ground walnuts and oats in fruit crisps.
- pureed vegetables and wheat germ in muffins.
- hidden veggies and beans in pasta with sauce.
- pureed fruit in homemade ice cream and frozen coffee drinks.
- pureed veggies and oat bran in corn bread.

Health Benefits of Method Ten

In this book, the ingredients I am adding are whole foods, so with this method you are adding fiber. The substitute you give him will not only supply him with the nutrients and antioxidants that are removed from processed foods, it will also make him feel full after eating so he won't overeat later. Including low-GI foods in recipes keeps the blood sugar levels balanced, reduces subsequent cravings for more sugar and the snacks that contain it, and has a positive influence on moods and concentration, among other things. Fiber also promotes regularity

and helps maintain healthy cholesterol and triglyceride levels.

Method Eleven
USE *VISUAL* DECOYS TO MAKE FOOD LOOK APPEALING

Some friends and I went to a restaurant the other night. When our dinners arrived, I noticed that each of us had a slight frown on our faces. We hadn't tasted a thing yet, but we weren't favorably disposed. Sure enough, each person said, "Well, I guess it tastes all right, but . . ." We couldn't put our finger on it, but something was wrong. Finally we figured out what it was. The yellow track lights over our heads made everything look old, not fresh. The meat looked as if it had been left out unrefrigerated. The vegetables and the sauces were brown and mousy. It was so off-putting that it was hard to ignore. The fact is, the track lights made our food taste bad.

Any chef at a four-star restaurant will tell you that presentation is everything. If the eyes tell you something looks good, you will assume it tastes good, too. I have even seen this in evidence at gourmet vegan restaurants with people who don't particularly like vegan food. The waiter sets a plate in front of the person. The layered raw vegetables look fresh and delicate. The combination of bright colors is enticing, and the crispy texture is unusually appealing. The person takes a single bite and savors it—all because of how it looks.

Method Eleven operates on this principle. The fact is that no matter how much you try to disguise it, as a Sneaky Chef, you are mucking around with your guy's food. If you are going to change the taste, even a little bit, you can often offset the results by making sure the food looks good. Think about color, texture, and shape to make the dish man-friendly. If your guy likes fried foods, how can you make the dish glisten as if it were laden with fat? If he likes a creamy texture, how can you create that effect without the heavy cream? If he likes sweets, how can you use just a little sugar on top to give the illusion of a sweeter dessert?

If you overlook this important step, you could be dooming your efforts to change his diet before they're even off the ground. Don't serve him his favorite chili obviously dotted with chunks of tofu, or his favorite corn bread now a muddy shade of brown from an overt switch to whole wheat.

A few examples of this method you will encounter in this book are:

- Dusting powdered sugar onto whole grain Legal Donuts, page 148, or Chocolate-Charged French Toast, page 154
- Scattering loveable chopped jalapeño peppers throughout whole grain veggie-loaded corn bread
- Using cocoa powder to hide the spinach/blueberry puree in Chocolate-Charged French Toast, page 154
- Serving a frozen coffee drink in a fun glass with a squirt of whipped cream
- Dusting sprinkles on sneaky chocolate-dipped strawberries
- Glazing sneaky meatloaf with ketchup or barbecue sauce
- Serving chicken satay on skewers
- Melting a little low-fat cheese over a crock of French onion soup loaded with vegetables

Desserts need special help when you're using healthier ingredients. After all, we *have to* eat dinner, but we only eat dessert because we *want to*. We're choosing pastries, pie, or pudding for pleasure. The whole idea of dessert is pleasure over substance. Eliminate the pleasure, and what's the point? If I'm going to ratchet down the sinful taste of a dessert, I employ a few decoys to distract from the healthy ingredients so my version looks just as good as its unhealthy counterpart.

The following tricks make healthy desserts appear more appealing:

- Mix (unmelted) chocolate chips into brownies to give the illusion of a richer dessert.
- Top low-fat cheesecake with a quick squirt of whipped cream.
- Dust powdered sugar on doughnuts and chocolate cookies.

We're all still young at heart. We want to be indulged, gratified, and satisfied when we eat, especially when it comes to dessert. In *The Sneaky Chef,* I tried to cater to children's inner passion to be "bad." Adults aren't that different. We're constantly tempted to eat precisely the foods our doctors tell us not to. If we're "good" for too long, we end up feeling deprived. And we can't be fooled about it.

I hear ultra-thin celebrities say that they're not on a diet. As they present it, it just so happens that they have gravitated towards eating steamed vegetables, no dairy, no carbs—forever. For dessert, they allow themselves one brownie a month. "It's a way of life," they say, "it's not a diet." But we all know it is. If we can't eat what we want, when we want, and as much as we want, then it's a diet.

"Anyhow, the hole in the doughnuts is at least digestible."

H.L. Mencken

This book caters to the honest truth that nobody wants to be on an endless diet. So we eat our dessert, but instead of it being the guiltiest dessert on the planet, we serve up a modified version. We use some sprinkles, a little bit of whipped cream, a dusting of powdered sugar, or a few chocolate chips to satisfy our desire. These are small indulgences that keep us on the right track without any sense of deprivation.

Health Benefits of Method Eleven

The decoys are not, in themselves, healthy, but their purpose is. You are using them to make the healthy ingredients go down well. You may experience a slight hesitation to using whipped cream and sprinkles, but remember that you're only adding a small amount. Think of it as a tiny payment for the greater good. If a mere five calories-worth of powdered sugar can trick your husband into eating an entire serving of fiber and vegetables in the form of a whole grain chocolate donut laced with wheat germ, spinach, and blueberries, then isn't it worth it? After all, he eats plenty of junk food with absolutely no health benefits.

Decoys are sometimes the one trick that makes a dish work, especially if your guy has a sensitive palate and notices every little difference in your cooking, or if he's the kind of guy who says, "That's not the way my mother used to make lasagna!" If you've changed the taste or the texture of a dish, there are times when the only way to make it work is to make it look not only delicious, but as close to the "same" as it always has looked.

Method Twelve
USE *FLAVOR* DECOYS TO DISTRACT GUYS FROM WHAT'S UNDERNEATH

I'm not suggesting that looks trump taste, just that looks help (especially with guys!). The new improved dish must be delicious, or your work as a Sneaky Chef has not been a success. You don't want your healthy ingredients to taste—god forbid!—healthy. You don't want an unpleasant or strange aftertaste. If your husband is eating with the guys, you don't want them to push your snacks aside and order pizza instead.

We've already established that the

sneaked foods in this book are superheroes that will keep your man in fine shape, but the ingredients used to fortify the recipes have to leave very little telltale taste of their own. I've tried every trick in the book, literally, to magically disguise the added ingredients, but sometimes there is a slightly different taste that just can't be gotten around. Our last trick is to use bold flavors that are great at masking any unavoidable off-tastes. Some of the favorites are:

- Chili pepper in veggie-laden chili
- Cayenne in calamari
- Jalapeños in whole grain corn bread
- Blue cheese in low-fat dressing
- Parmesan cheese on low-fat mashed potatoes
- Chipotle peppers in healthy hummus dip
- Garlic in Caesar dressing
- Dark chocolate in sneaky brownies
- Coffee in milkshakes
- Barbecue sauce in high-fiber meatloaf
- Bacon bits in corn chowder
- Horseradish in better Bloody Marys

The principle here is the same one all of our mothers employed when getting us to take our medicine as youngsters. Remember the old phrase, "A spoonful of honey makes the medicine go down"? Mom either buried the bitter cough syrup in honey, or she bought a brand that was cherry- or orange-flavored. We have to do a lot better than that with our recipes, though, because that tablespoon of cough syrup still tasted like medicine. It's not as if she was fooling us. We, on the other hand, really are trying to fool our guys into thinking these are their favorite dishes, just as they've always had them before.

Method Twelve deceives the tongue and distracts your guy from perceiving any new or off-flavors that sometimes bleed through from the healthy ingredients in the recipe. The flavors listed above are bold enough to overpower most foods. The idea is for the guy to immediately pick up on the tastes he is accustomed to, like cayenne or chili powder, and quickly forget about the slight peculiarity. And I do mean "slight." If the discrepancy is strong, this trick won't work.

Health Benefits
of Method Twelve

The health benefits of this method are essentially the same as in Method Eleven. We use a small amount of a flavor we know our guy is attracted to so he'll eat the healthy ingredients he *isn't* attracted to at all. Packaged goods may use the same idea, but they often go into overkill. They add too much sugar or salt or some artificial cheese flavoring just to lure the consumer into purchasing their product. We can do better. When we're in the kitchen, we can control how much of the decoy food is added to the dish. Often, it is a fraction of what the food giants use, and we strictly limit saturated fats. Our reasons for using the decoy in the first place are the right reasons—we're not trying to sell anybody on anything. We're just trying to get our guys to eat nature's superfoods so we can keep them in good shape. Our muffins, with their seemingly sinful decoy ingredients, still have more nutritional punch than Hostess Twinkies!

Method Thirteen
USE FRIENDLY *TEXTURE* DECOYS

Inexperienced cooks often forget to be concerned with the texture of foods, whereas experienced cooks know that texture is almost as important as taste. Here are some key words that indicate texture: *crunchy, creamy, gritty, heavy, crispy, frothy, chewy, frizzy, juicy, buttery, delicate, grainy, smooth, soft, light, firm, silky, tender, fluffy, stringy, oily,* and *bubbly .*

Texture can do a great deal for a dish. Sometimes all a dessert needs, for example, is a few nuts, not because of the taste, but because they make it crunchy. On the other hand, the wrong texture can ruin a dish; consider lumpy mayonnaise or a gritty soufflé. A sauce might look and taste great, but if it is grainy when it ought to be smooth, it won't go over well with the fellas.

I have discovered a few simple, highly effective ways to change the texture of a recipe so it appeals to every diner. Some of these ingredients we have mentioned before. They tend to pull double duty.

- When you add spinach to chocolate-dipped strawberries (yes, this is possible!), dust them with sprinkles or chopped nuts.
- When you add spinach and blueberries to brownies, add in some chopped walnuts.
- When you add wheat germ and ricotta to pancakes, mix in a few chocolate chips.
- When you add cauliflower to mashed potatoes, mix in a few bacon bits.
- When you add tofu to fettuccine Alfredo, add in a few bacon bits.

Here's the problem: One of the main detractions of vegetables and whole grains and other natural foods just happens to be their texture. For whatever reason, we have been taught to dislike the grainy, gritty texture. Instead, we often prefer artificially fluffed up foods. This means that a lot of the ingredients you and I are trying to sneak into our men's dishes are precisely the ones that will add a texture that turns them off. We have to be very creative here because we are trying to cover up a multitude of "sins."

I often use crunchiness in my recipes to cover an unwanted taste or a slightly unfavorable texture because people don't pay attention to what's underneath the crunch. You can, however, even think of Method One as a texture decoy in certain recipes. After all, one reason for pureeing spinach and other vegetables in the first place is that men don't like their texture. Pureeing makes them smooth and pudding-like, and therefore acceptable. In some dishes I accomplish the same thing by adding extra cheese to make it creamier.

Health Benefits of Method Thirteen

This method simply increases the odds that when you place your carefully prepared dish on the table, he will chow it down. The number of calories added by the decoys is minimal, yet they act as a great lure. This gives you the freedom to add even more healthy ingredients to your recipes.

CHAPTER FIVE

Make-Ahead Recipes & Glossary of Superfoods

Now that we have gone through the sneaky chef's indispensable bag of tricks, let's put these clever methods into action.

This might be hard to believe, but after my first book was published, people kept asking me one hilarious question about the Make-Ahead recipes: "Can you make these ahead of time?" That's like asking a racecar driver if he goes fast. When the word *race* is in the job title, you pretty much have your answer. The Make-Ahead recipes are the key to making my methods accessible and efficient. For best results, you'll want to front-load a little extra work, probably at the beginning of each week, so you can quickly whip up the rest of the life-enhancing recipes for the rest of the week. You're investing about thirty minutes to combine a few super-ingredients that will amplify the health effects of an otherwise ordinary dish. Whenever you need the Make-Aheads, just pull the container out of the refrigerator, and Bingo! Instant nutrition.

Using Make-Ahead recipes embodies my whole philosophy about cooking: "It shouldn't be hard and it shouldn't eat up your time." Naturally it took me time to figure out how to save time, but after years in the kitchen, I finally came up with a strategy that worked. I know there are busy wives and mothers just like me all over the country who want to cook for their families without returning to the nineteenth century, when cooking took up a woman's entire day. But there are a few aspects of the twenty-first century that many of us don't want to hold onto, either, like resorting to frozen dinners, fast food, and pizza delivery. This habit has resulted in too many obese children and husbands with their guts hanging over their belts. Becoming a Sneaky Chef is the simplest way I know to have the best of both worlds.

All of the following purees and juices can be stored in the refrigerator for up to three days, and in the freezer for up to three months. As I said earlier, you will find it ex-

traordinarily convenient to open the freezer and take out two baggies containing a half a cup of puree, just the amount you need for your recipe.

Make-Ahead Recipe #1: Purple Puree

3 cups raw baby spinach
   leaves
1½ cups fresh or frozen
   blueberries, no syrup
   or sugar added
½ teaspoon lemon juice
1 to 2 tablespoons water

MAKES ABOUT 1 CUP OF PUREE

Thoroughly wash the spinach, even if the package says "pre-washed." If using frozen blueberries, quickly rinse them under cold water to thaw a little, and then drain.

Fill the bowl of your food processor with the spinach, blueberries, lemon juice, and 1 tablespoon of water; puree on high until as smooth as possible. Stop occasionally to push the contents to the bottom. If necessary, use another tablespoon of water to smooth-out the puree.

This recipe makes about 1 cup of puree; double it if you want to store another cup. It will keep in the refrigerator up to 3 days, or you can freeze ¼-cup portions in sealed plastic bags or small plastic containers.

Purple Puree is used in the following recipes:

Legal Donuts
Power Breakfast Cookies
Chocolate-Charged French Toast
Sneak-a-Chinos
BBQ Maximum Meatloaf

Barbell Burgers
Chocolate-Dipped Strawberries
Brawny Brownies
Vulcan Molten Chocolate Cake

Make-Ahead Recipe #2: Orange Puree

1 medium sweet potato
or yam, peeled and
coarsely chopped

3 medium to large carrots,
peeled and sliced into
thick chunks

2 to 3 tablespoons water

MAKES ABOUT 2 CUPS OF PUREE

In a medium-sized pot, cover the sweet potatoes and carrots with cold water and boil for about 20 minutes, until carrots are very tender. If the carrots aren't thoroughly cooked, they'll leave tell-tale little nuggets of vegetables in recipes, which will reveal their presence to your man—a gigantic no-no for the Sneaky Chef.

Drain the sweet potatoes and carrots and put them in the food processor with two tablespoons of water. Puree on high until smooth; no pieces of carrots or potatoes should remain. Stop occasionally to push the contents to the bottom. If necessary, use another tablespoon of water to smooth out the puree, but the less water, the better.

This recipe makes about 2 cups of puree; double it if you want to store another 2 cups. It will keep in the refrigerator for up to 3 days, or you can freeze $\frac{1}{4}$-cup portions in sealed plastic bags or small plastic containers.

Orange Puree is used in the following recipes:

Top Banana Waffles

Bonanza Crunch Muffins

Quick Fixes for Condiments

Revamped Reuben

Beefed-Up Onion Soup

Manhattan Clam Chowder

Quick Fixes for Canned Baked Beans

Quick Fixes for Store-Bought Salsa

Homemade BBQ Sauce

Quick Fixes for Store-Bought Barbecue
   Sauce

Mega Marinara Sauce

Quick Fixes for Store-Bought Tomato
   Sauce

Sweet and Sour Sauce

Fearless Fried Chicken

Quick Fixes for a Manwich®

Perfecto Parmigiano

Bowling-Night Bolognese

Everybody Loves Romano Chicken

Linguine with Red Clam Sauce

Something's Fishy Sticks

Charmin' Chicken Parm

Gone Fishin' Salmon Burgers

Grilled Chicken Satay with Peanut
   Dipping Sauce

Make-Ahead Recipe #3: Green Puree

2 cups raw baby spinach
leaves

2 cups broccoli florets,
fresh or frozen

1 cup sweet green peas,
frozen

2 to 3 tablespoons water

MAKES ABOUT 2 CUPS OF PUREE

If using raw spinach, thoroughly wash it, even if the package says "prewashed."

To prepare on the stovetop, pour about 2 inches of water into a pot with a tight-fitting lid. Put a vegetable steamer basket into the pot, add the spinach and broccoli, and steam for about 10 minutes, until very tender. Add the frozen peas to the basket for the last 2 minutes of steaming. Drain.

To prepare in the microwave, place the broccoli and spinach in a microwave-safe bowl, cover with water, and microwave on high for 8 to 10 minutes, until very tender. Add peas for last 2 minutes of cooking. Drain.

Place the vegetables in the bowl of your food processor along with 2 tablespoons of water. Puree on high until as smooth as possible. Stop occasionally to push the contents to the bottom. If necessary, use another tablespoon of water to smooth out the puree.

This recipe makes about 2 cups of puree; double it if you want to store another 2 cups. It will keep in the refrigerator for up to 3 days, or you can freeze $\frac{1}{4}$-cup portions in sealed plastic bags or small plastic containers.

Green Puree is used in the following recipes:

Quick Fixes for Condiments

Perfect Pesto

Pesto Mashed Potatoes

Perfecto Parmigiano

Bowling-Night Bolognese

Real Man Meatballs

Doctor's Choice Chili

Pizza Pesto

One-and-Only Guacamole

Quick Fixes for Store-Bought Guacamole

Make-Ahead Recipe #4: White Puree

2 cups cauliflower florets
   (about ½ a small head)
2 small to medium
   zucchini, peeled and
   coarsely chopped
1 teaspoon fresh lemon
   juice
1 to 2 tablespoons water,
   if necessary

MAKES ABOUT 2 CUPS OF PUREE

Pour about 2 inches of water into a pot with a tight-fitting lid. Put a vegetable steamer basket into the pot, add the cauliflower, and steam for 10 to 12 minutes or until very tender. Drain. Alternatively, place the cauliflower in a microwave-safe bowl, cover the cauliflower with water, and microwave on high for 8 to 10 minutes or until very tender. Drain.

While cauliflower steams, pulse the *raw* peeled zucchini with the lemon juice (no water at this point) in your food processor. Once the cauliflower is cooked and tender, working in batches if necessary, add 1 tablespoon of water and some of the cauliflower to the food processor with the pulsed zucchini. Puree on high until smooth. Stop occasionally to push the contents to the bottom. If necessary, use another tablespoon of water to smooth out the puree, but the less water, the better.

This recipe makes about 2 cups of puree; double it if you want to store another 2 cups. It will keep in the refrigerator for up to 3 days, or you can freeze ¼-cup portions in sealed plastic bags or small plastic containers.

White Puree is used in the following recipes:

Refried Bean Macho Nachos

Mega Marinara Sauce

Quick Fixes for Store-Bought Tomato
   Sauce

Mighty Mashed Potatoes, 5 Sneaky Ways

Charmin' Chicken Parm

Perfecto Parmigiano

Everybody Loves Romano Chicken

Better Batter Onion Rings

Don't-Be-Sorry Calamari

Grilled Corn Bread

Homemade BBQ Sauce

Hungry Man Hummus

Boosted Buffalo Wings Wrap

Burly Burrito

Plenty of Polenta

Blastin' Bean Dip

Don't Fret Fritters

Doctor's Choice Chili

White Lie Spaghetti Pie

Stuffed Manli-Cotti

Cold Sesame Noodles

Bountiful Blue Cheese Dressing

Boosted Buffalo Wings

Quick Fixes for a Manwich

Quick Fixes for Condiments

Major Leek Soup

Bloody Mary, "A Salad in a Glass"

Quick Fixes for Store-Bought Barbecue
   Sauce

Quick Fixes for Store-Bought Salsa

Manhattan Clam Chowder

Quick Fixes for Canned Baked Beans

Fearless Fried Chicken

Something's Fishy Sticks

Make-Ahead Recipe #5: Green Juice

3 cups raw baby spinach
    leaves

1 cup water

MAKES ABOUT 1 CUP OF JUICE

Thoroughly wash the spinach, even if the package says "pre-washed." In a medium-sized pot, heat the spinach and the water to a boil; reduce the heat to low and simmer for 10 minutes. Pour into a fine mesh strainer over a container or bowl, pressing the green "pulp" with the back of a spoon until all the liquid is released.

This recipe makes about 1 cup of juice; double it if you want to store another cup. It will keep in the refrigerator for up to 3 days, or you can freeze $\frac{1}{4}$-cup portions in sealed plastic bags or small plastic containers.

Green Juice is used in the following recipes:

Quick Fixes for Store-Bought Barbecue
    Sauce

Minty Hot Cocoa

Make-Ahead Recipe #6: Blueberry Juice

$2\frac{1}{2}$ cups fresh or frozen
blueberries, no syrup
or sugar added

2 cups water

1 tablespoon sugar

MAKES 2 CUPS OF JUICE

In a medium-sized pot, heat the blueberries, water, and sugar to a boil; reduce heat to low and simmer for 10 minutes, occasionally mashing the blueberries with the back of a spoon to release their juices. Pour the cooked mixture into a fine mesh strainer over a container or bowl, pressing the blueberry "pulp" with the back of a spoon until all the liquid is released.

This recipe makes 2 cups of juice; double it if you want to store another 2 cups. This recipe also yields about $\frac{3}{4}$ cup of leftover pulp in the strainer; save this pulp to add to the Purple Puree, page 99.

Store in the refrigerator for up to 3 days, or freeze $\frac{1}{4}$-cup portions in sealed plastic bags or small plastic containers.

Blueberry Juice is used in the following recipes:

Quick Fixes for Store-Bought Barbecue
    Sauce

My Sweetheart-Tini

Make-Ahead Recipe #7: Cherry Juice

$2\frac{1}{2}$ cups fresh or frozen
  pitted cherries,* no
  syrup or sugar added
2 cups water
1 tablespoon sugar

*Try to use **organic** cherries, since they rank high on the "dirty dozen" list of produce most contaminated with pesticide residues.*

MAKES ABOUT 2 CUPS OF JUICE

In a medium-sized pot, heat the cherries, water, and sugar to a boil; reduce heat to low and simmer for 10 minutes, occasionally mashing the cherries with the back of a spoon or a potato masher to release their juices. Pour the cooked cherries into a fine mesh strainer over a container or bowl, pressing the cherry "pulp" with the back of a spoon until all the liquid is released.

This recipe makes 2 cups of juice; double it if you want to store another 2 cups. This recipe also yields about $\frac{3}{4}$ cup of leftover pulp in the strainer; save this pulp to add to the Cherry Smoothie, page 167.

Store in the refrigerator for up to 3 days, or freeze $\frac{1}{4}$-cup portions in sealed plastic bags or small plastic containers.

Cherry Juice is used in the following recipes:

Cherry Vanilla Martini
Minty Hot Cocoa

Make-Ahead Recipe #8: Strawberry Juice

$2\frac{1}{2}$ cups fresh or frozen
strawberries,* no syrup
or sugar added

2 cups water

1 tablespoon sugar

*Try to use **organic** strawberries, since they rank high on the "dirty dozen" list of produce most contaminated with pesticide residues.*

MAKES 2 CUPS OF JUICE

In a medium-sized pot, heat the strawberries, water, and sugar to a boil; reduce heat to low and simmer for 10 minutes, occasionally mashing the strawberries with the back of a spoon to release their juices. Pour the cooked berries into a fine mesh strainer over a container or bowl, pressing the strawberry "pulp" with the back of a spoon until all the liquid is released.

This recipe makes 2 cups of juice; double it if you want to store another 2 cups. This recipe also yields about $\frac{3}{4}$ cup of leftover pulp in the strainer; save this pulp to add to the Strawberry Smoothie, page 167.

Store in refrigerator for up to 3 days, or freeze $\frac{1}{4}$-cup portions in sealed plastic bags or small plastic containers.

Strawberry Juice is used in the following recipes:

Quick Fixes for Store-Bought Barbecue
    Sauce

My Sweetheart-Tini

Make-Ahead Recipe #9: White Bean Puree

1 (15-ounce) can white beans* (Great Northern, navy, butter, or cannellini)

1 to 2 tablespoons water

If you are starting with dry beans, soak 1 cup for an hour, then cook according to instructions.

MAKES ABOUT 1 CUP OF PUREE

Rinse and drain the beans and put them into the bowl of your food processor. Add 1 tablespoon of the water, then pulse several times to puree, stopping occasionally to scrape the contents to the bottom. The goal is a smooth, but **not wet**, puree, about the consistency of peanut butter. If necessary, use a little more water, one teaspoonful at a time, to smooth-out the puree until there are no flecks of whole beans visible.

This recipe makes about 1 cup of puree; double it if you want to store another cup. It will keep in the refrigerator for up to 3 days, or you can freeze $\frac{1}{4}$-cup portions in sealed plastic bags or small plastic containers.

White Bean Puree is used in the following recipes:

Quick Fixes for Store-Bought Guacamole

Quick Fixes for Store-Bought Tomato Sauce

Tricky Tuna Sandwich

Egg-Me-On Salad Sandwich

Mighty Mashed Potatoes, 5 Sneaky Ways

Green Tea and White Bean Creamy Vinaigrette

Rosemary-Olive Biscotti

Heartichoke Dip

Blockbuster Blueberry Muffins

Hobo Hash

Hash Brown Patties

Not His Mother's Meatloaf

Now You're Talkin' Turkey Burgers

Concealed Crab Cakes

Quick Fixes for a Manwich

Chicken Waldorf Wrap

Quick Fixes for Condiments

Side of Slaw

Tailgate Turkey Slaw Wrap

Packed Potato Salad

Not-for-Chicks Chicken Salad

Chow Down Chowder

Quick Fixes for Store-Bought Barbecue
   Sauce

Your Honey's Mustard Sauce/Dip

Make-Ahead Recipe #10: Chickpea Puree

1 (15-ounce) can chickpeas*
   (garbanzo beans)
2 to 3 tablespoons water

If you prefer to use dry beans, soak overnight and cook as directed.

MAKES ABOUT 1 CUP OF PUREE

Rinse and drain the chickpeas and put them into the bowl of your food processor. Add 1 tablespoon of the water, then pulse several times to puree, stopping occasionally to scrape the contents to the bottom. The goal is a smooth, but **not wet,** puree. If necessary, use a little more water, one teaspoonful at a time, to smooth out the puree until there are no more flecks of full chickpeas visible.

This recipe makes about 1 cup of puree; double it if you want to store another cup. It will keep in the refrigerator for up to 3 days, or you can freeze $\frac{1}{4}$-cup portions in sealed plastic bags or small plastic containers.

Chickpea Puree is used in the following recipes:

Rosemary Olive Biscotti

SINLESS SMOOTHIES

Sneaky Ingredients: Avocado, Pomegranate juice, Green tea, Blueberries, Strawberries (with banana), Cherries

**STACKED
BLUEBERRY
PANCAKES**

Sneaky Ingredients:

Ricotta

Oat Bran

Almonds

LEGAL DONUTS

Sneaky Ingredients:

Blueberries

Spinach

Wheat Germ

BLOCKBUSTER BLUEBERRY MUFFINS

Sneaky Ingredients: White beans, Wheat germ, Oat bran

SNEAK-A-CHINO (MOCHA FLAVOR)

Sneaky Ingredients: Avocado

BEEFED UP ONION SOUP

Sneaky Ingredients:
Pomegranate juice
Sweet potatoes
Carrots

MANHATTAN CLAM CHOWDER

Sneaky Ingredients:
Cauliflower
Zucchini
Sweet Potatoes
Carrots
Sardines

SUPER BOWL PARTY

HUNGRY-MAN HUMMUS
Sneaky Ingredients: Tofu, Cauliflower, Zucchini

HEARTICHOKE DIP
Sneaky Ingredients: White Beans Wheat Germ

REFRIED BEAN MACHO NACHOS
Sneaky Ingredients: Cauliflower Zucchini

SPICE BOYS CORN CHIPS

SUPER BOWL OF NUTS

TRICKY TUNA SANDWICH
Sneaky Ingredients: Sardines, White beans, Oat bran

REVAMPED REUBEN

Sneaky Ingredients: Sweet potatoes, Carrots

**EGG-ME-ON
SALAD
SANDWICH**

Sneaky Ingredients:
Tofu
White beans

**QUICK FIXES FOR
CONDIMENTS (FROM
LEFT, CLOCKWISE):**

Sneaky Ingredients:
Ketchup (with Orange
Puree)
Green Goddess (with
Green Puree)
BBQ Sauce (with White
Puree)
Cranberry Relish (with
Orange Puree)
Mustard (with White Bean
Puree)
Salsa (with Orange Puree)
Mayonnaise (with White
Bean Puree)

Make-Ahead Recipe #11: Frozen Bananas

Ripe bananas

Use bananas that are overripe and speckled with brown spots—they have more natural sugars in them at this stage. Peel and break each one into 3 or 4 pieces. Freeze in sealed plastic bags to use in shakes and other recipes.

Frozen Bananas are used in the following recipes:

Fuel Good Meal Replacement Shakes

Sinless Smoothies

Ice Cream, 3 Sneaky Ways

Make-Ahead Recipe #12: Better Breading

1 cup almonds, slivered
and blanched (optional,
omit if allergic)

1 cup bread crumbs,
preferably whole wheat*

1 cup wheat germ,
unsweetened

1 teaspoon salt

MAKES 3 CUPS OF BREADING

Pulse the almonds in a food processor. Don't let the food processor run continually, or you will end up with nut butter. You are aiming for the consistency of cornmeal, not bread flour.

Pour the almond meal into a large bowl. Add the bread crumbs, wheat germ, and salt. Whisk to combine.

Refrigerate in a sealed, labeled plastic bag for up to 2 weeks.

Sneaky Tip:

*Whole wheat bread crumbs can be found in natural and organic food stores, but you can easily make your own. Just pulse whole grain bread in a food processor to achieve fine crumbs. It's that simple. Three slices of bread yield about one cup of fresh crumbs. They keep for weeks in a sealed plastic bag or container in the freezer.

Better Breading is used in the following recipes:

Perfecto Parmigiano   Something's Fishy Sticks

Make-Ahead Recipe #13: Flour Blend

1 cup all-purpose,
   unbleached white flour

1 cup whole wheat flour

1 cup wheat germ,
   unsweetened

MAKES 3 CUPS OF FLOUR BLEND

Combine the flours and wheat germ in a large bowl.

This blend can be stored in a sealed, labeled plastic bag or container in the refrigerator for up to 3 months.

Sneaky Tip:

A quick replacement for my Flour Blend is Eagle Mills All-Purpose Flour made with Ultragrain®. It's already blended for you! Cup for cup, you'll get more whole grain nutrition than in white flour—with the great taste, color, and texture you expect.

Flour Blend is used in the following recipes:

Legal Donuts

Power Breakfast Cookies

Cinnamon Toast Breakfast Biscotti

Top Banana Waffles

Wiley Walnut Waffles

Blockbuster Blueberry Muffins

Bonanza Crunch Muffins

Rosemary-Olive Biscotti

Grilled Corn Bread

Brawny Brownies

Feel-Good Fruit Crisp Topping

Hi-Fi Pie Crust

Vulcan Molten Chocolate Cake

Make-Ahead Recipe #14: Ground Almonds

1 cup almonds, slivered
and blanched

MAKES 1 CUP

Pulse the almonds in a food processor. Don't let the food processor run continually, or you will end up with nut butter. You are aiming for the consistency of cornmeal, not bread flour.

Keep refrigerated in a sealed, labeled plastic bag for up to 2 weeks.

Ground Almonds are used in the following recipes:

Well-Stacked Pancakes

Side of Slaw

Tailgate Turkey Slaw Wrap

Better Batter Onion Rings

Don't-Be-Sorry Calamari

Baked Clams

Fearless Fried Chicken

Chocolate-Dipped Strawberries

Make-Ahead Recipe #15: Ground Walnuts

1 cup shelled walnut halves
or pieces

MAKES 1 CUP

Pulse the walnuts in a food processor. Don't let the food processor run continually, or you will end up with nut butter. You are aiming for the consistency of cornmeal, not bread flour.

Keep refrigerated in a sealed, labeled plastic bag for up to 2 weeks.

Ground Walnuts are used in the following recipes:

Power Breakfast Cookies

Cinnamon Toast Breakfast Biscotti

Top Banana Waffles

Wiley Walnut Waffles

Bonanza Crunch Muffins

Chicken Waldorf Wrap

Perfect Pesto

Gone Fishin' Salmon Burgers
(walnut crusted variation)

Super Bowl of Nuts

Chocolate-Dipped Strawberries

Brawny Brownies

Feel-Good Fruit Crisp Topping

Hi-Fi Pie Crust

Make-Ahead Recipe #16: Bacon Bits

1 pound turkey bacon,
    cut into $\frac{1}{2}$-inch pieces

MAKES APPROXIMATELY 3 CUPS

Fry the bacon (or cook it in the microwave) until it is crisp. Cool. Blot with a paper towel to absorb any excess oil. Crumble and store in a sealed plastic bag in the refrigerator for up to 3 days or in the freezer for 3 months.

Sneaky Tip:

You can substitute vegetarian (soy) bacon bits or packaged bacon bits (ideally with no nitrates) in place of this recipe.

Bacon Bits are used in the following recipes:

Major Leek Soup

Bacon-and-Cheddar Mashed Potatoes

Baked Clams

Steakhouse Salad with Blue Cheese
    and Bacon

Fettuccine Don't Be Afraid-O

Grilled Corn Bread

INSTANT SUPERMARKET PUREES

If you don't have time, or don't want to puree, you can become an instant Sneaky Chef by using jarred baby food as a convenient alternative for many of the fruits and vegetables you'll be adding to your man's (macho!) meals. It sounds a little funny at first, but it makes perfect sense when you think about it: where else can you find a ready-made source of all natural, highest quality fruit and vegetable purees? Forget about the baby food label, we're talking about top quality purees here. I've discovered that Beech-Nut® brand baby food in particular has extremely high quality standards. Unlike other large company brands—

Sneaky Tip:

Other useful instant supermarket purees are tomato paste, applesauce, unsweetened fruit spread, and fresh, ripe avocados (mashed).

even organic lines—their purees contain no sugar, modified food starch, thickeners or other additives. What's more, you don't have to go to a specialty food store to find Beech-Nut—it's widely distributed in the U.S., and can be found in most supermarkets across the country. What better way to baby your man? These purees most closely match my homemade purees in taste, texture, and color. Just don't let him see the jars!

GLOSSARY OF SUPERFOODS

Please note: This glossary is meant for informational purposes only. If you have questions about your health, consult your personal physician.

ALMONDS

At first glance, these tree nuts may appear to be high in fat, but like the fat in olive oil, it's all the good kind (monounsaturated, which can help lower cholesterol, protect against heart disease, and even help prevent cancer. Almonds contain arginine, an amino acid that is converted to nitric oxide (similar to nitroglycerin) in the body, which can help keep blood platelets from clumping. Almonds are

MAKE AHEAD	INGREDIENTS	INSTANT SUBSTITUTE
White Puree	cauliflower/zucchini	baby food zucchini
Orange Puree	sweet potatoes/carrots	baby food sweet potatoes and carrots
Green Puree	peas, broccoli, spinach	baby food peas, spinach, vegetables
Purple Puree	blueberries/spinach	baby food apples and blueberries with baby food spinach
White Bean Puree	white beans	vegetarian refried pinto beans (these are darker in color, and not as bland as white beans—they will work only with darker-colored meat and tomato sauce)
Blueberry Juice	blueberries	bottled blueberry or pomegranate juice
Strawberry Juice	strawberries	bottled strawberry or pomegranate juice
Cherry Juice	cherries	bottled cherry or pomegranate juice
Green Juice	spinach	spinach juice from a health food store or juice bar

also high in antioxidant-laden vitamin E and magnesium, which improve blood flow and keep arteries and veins open. Just a quarter cup of almonds boasts more protein than an egg. Research also shows that pairing almonds with foods high in sugar and other simple carbohydrates will help to reduce the increase in blood sugar that would normally occur after eating those foods—making them a great ice cream topping!

AVOCADO

Called one of the most nutritious fruits on Earth (yes, it's a fruit), avocados are nearly a complete food. According to noted food writer Gaylord Hauser, "In this single delectable fruit are combined the protein of meat, the fat of butter [but much more wholesome!], the vitamins and minerals of green vegetables, the flavor of nuts, a six course dinner." Avocados contain nearly twenty vitamins, minerals, and phytonutrients and are particularly loaded with vitamins C and E, iron, fiber and lutein, which is important for eye health. Avocados contain omega-3 fatty acids and oleic acid, a monounsaturated fat that may help lower cholesterol. They're a good source of potassium, which helps reg-

ulate blood pressure, and folate, a nutrient important for heart health. Avocados also increase your body's ability to absorb the nutrients that other vegetables provide, so toss some into your salad.

BANANAS

Bananas are nature's best source of potassium, an essential mineral for maintaining normal blood pressure and heart function. They can help decrease the risk of stroke, lower high blood pressure, relieve heartburn, prevent ulcers, and speed the recovery from diarrhea. Bananas have long been recognized for their antacid effects, which protects against stomach ulcers and helps to restore electrolytes after dehydration caused by stomach illness. They also add pectin, a soluble beneficial fiber that can help normalize movement through the digestive tract and ease constipation. As if that weren't enough, bananas nourish the "good" bacteria in the colon that promote wholesome digestion and strengthen the immune system. Bananas are believed to prevent the oxidation of dangerous low-density lipoprotein, a process that causes it to stick to the walls of the arteries. This accumulation can contribute to atherosclerosis, or hardening of the arteries, a major contributor to heart attack, stroke, and high blood pressure. Even one daily serving of a potassium rich food like bananas can lower your risk of stroke by up to 40 percent.

BLUEBERRIES

Blueberries are much more than just a delicious dessert. Researchers at the USDA have ranked blueberries first in antioxidants (which slow aging by helping to destroy free radicals) in comparison to all other fresh fruits! They can help prevent cataracts, ward off cancer, reduce inflammation, relieve constipation, improve brain function, and reduce the risk of infection. They can help prevent cellular changes that lead to cancer, and they're touted to be even more effective than red wine at providing cardiovascular benefits from their high antioxidant content. Blueberries are low in calories and rich in soluble fiber, which helps reduce cholesterol. Their high vitamin C content helps prevent infections and especially helps prevent cataracts and age-related macular degeneration, the primary cause of vision loss in older adults. Blueberries contain a rare chemical called

pterostilbene that can help protect the brain from oxidative stress and may reduce the effects of age-related conditions such as Alzheimer's disease or dementia. Studies have also indicated that pterostilbene may help prevent colon cancer by lowering cholesterol in the body.

BROCCOLI

Broccoli is a member of the cabbage family and is closely related to cauliflower. It is difficult to overestimate broccoli's health benefits. It contains indole-3-carbinol and sulforaphane, both protective against cancers, especially of the breast, colon, and prostate. It is high in beta-carotene and a variety of other nutrients, including calcium, folate, fiber, and vitamins C and K, which fortify the immune system and can help ward off many other conditions, from heart disease to osteoporosis and diabetes. Sneaky Chef recipes like Real Man Meatballs, page 259, combine broccoli with tomatoes, which, when eaten together, have a synergistic effect that provides better protection against cancer than when eaten separately. A recent study also provides support for broccoli's ability to eliminate

Helicobacter pylori (H. pylori), a primary cause of stomach ulcers.

CARROTS

When it comes to vegetables, the brighter the color, the greater its health benefits, so the orange in carrots are a clue to their many sterling health qualities. Known as the "king of vegetables," carrots are the richest source of carotenes and antioxidants among them all. Vitamin A–rich foods like carrots have been found to protect smokers (and those exposed to secondhand smoke) from emphysema and other smoking-related illnesses. In fact, some studies have shown that as little as one carrot per day could cut the risk of lung cancer in half. Carotenoids may also be beneficial to blood sugar regulation, especially helpful today due to the prevalence of packaged carbs and sugary snack foods. Rich in beta- and alpha-carotene (which convert to Vitamin A in the body), carrots can help improve vision in general, but especially night vision; beta-carotene can also help repair tissue damaged by rigorous exercise. Because they contain soluble fiber, they also help lower cholesterol and reduce the risk of cancer and heart disease.

CAULIFLOWER

Cauliflower, a member of the cruciferous family, can help inhibit tumor growth and boost the immune system almost as well as its darker-hued cousin, broccoli. Its cancer-fighting arsenal includes allicin, selenium, and the phytonutrients sulforaphane and indole-3-carbinol, all of which aid in the prevention of cancers of the colon, breast, and prostate. Cauliflower is high in both vitamin C and folate, which not only strengthen the immune system, they also help prevent anemia, are essential for normal tissue growth, and can increase male fertility. Cauliflower is an excellent source of fiber, which improves colon health and can also help to maintain a healthy cholesterol level.

CHERRY JUICE

Often referred to as the "healing fruit," cherries are among the ten highest-rated fruits for antioxidants, which can help slow the aging process, as well as vitamins A, C, potassium, fiber, flavonoids, and ellagic acid, which are all powerful anti-cancer agents. Studies have shown that cherries, especially the tart ones, can help reduce inflammation in the body, reducing the risk of heart disease and stroke. This same property can help to eliminate migraine headaches, similar to aspirin or ibuprofen. Cherries are rich in melatonin, the naturally-occurring hormone that has been found to slow aging and enhance sleep. They are also high in the flavonoid quercetin, known for its potential health benefits, including its role in blood clotting and reducing the risk for heart attack and stroke.

CHILI POWDER (AND CAYENNE)

This hot spice contains a substance called capsaicin, which reduces blood cholesterol, triglyceride levels, platelet clumping, and inflammation. It's also a natural pain reliever and has been useful in relieving arthritis. The hotter the chile pepper, the more capsaicin it contains. Chili powder can help clear mucus from your nose and/or congested lungs and boost immunity through beta-carotene and vitamins C and A. It may help stop the spread of prostate cancer, prevent stomach ulcers, and assist with weight reduction.

And one last note: don't fall for the old trick of taking a bite from a hot chile pepper after someone else has shown you that it's "re- *ally not hot" by taking the first bite. The heat of the pepper isn't found in the tip—it begins about a third of the way up, so the first bite is barely hot at all, but the rest can be fiery!*

CHOCOLATE AND COCOA

The health benefits of chocolate are the best news to hit the health scene since pizza! Modern science claims that cocoa and dark chocolate, the product made from it, is good for the arteries, protects your skin from sun- and age-damage, and has nearly twice the antioxidants of red wine and green tea. On the Oxygen Radical Absorbance Capacity (ORAC) scale, which measures the antioxidant power of foods, cocoa outranks even all-star blueberries! Cocoa's high serotonin levels aid relaxation and act as a stress reducer. New research shows a bite of chocolate a day may lower blood pressure and bad cholesterol, increase good cholesterol, and inhibit blood clotting. The phytosterols (plant-based compounds) abundant in cocoa are responsible for these good effects. The only disclaimer: limit yourself to just a few bites a day. Due to the high sugar and fat content of most dark chocolate bars, less is more.

CINNAMON

This warming spice shows anti-clotting and cholesterol lowering properties. The essential oil cinnamaldehyde in cinnamon helps prevent unwanted clumping of blood platelets by inhibiting the release of an inflammatory agent called arachidonic acid. The Diabetic Association has acknowledged cinnamon's ability to reduce blood sugar levels and prevent the onset of adult type 2 diabetes; as little as half a teaspoon per day can lower blood sugar levels an average of 20 percent in only a few weeks. Cinnamon also stimulates circulation, aids digestion, staves off hunger, relieves gas, and fights colds, coughs, and fevers. Its smell alone can produce positive effects on brain function.

CUMIN

Cumin contains minerals like manganese, magnesium, potassium, calcium, and significant amounts of iron, which is excellent for energy and immune function. Cumin may also aid in digestion, and its anti-carcinogenic properties may help protect against stomach and liver tumors. Cumin also contains a phytochemical called limolene that may play a role in cancer prevention, specifically prostate cancer.

GARLIC

One of the greatest benefits of garlic is that it's a natural antibiotic that strengthens the body's overall immune system and helps prevent colds and the flu. There is increasing evidence that the sulfur compounds in garlic may reduce triglycerides, cholesterol, blood pressure, and blood sugar; decrease the risk of stomach and colon cancer; thin the blood to help prevent heart disease and stroke; and relieve asthma.

GINGER

Next time you're on a cruise, try some ginger! Studies have shown ginger to be superior to over-the-counter and prescription drugs for motion sickness. Traditional Chinese medicine relies on ginger to soothe nausea and stop diarrhea. Its nausea-fighting properties make it helpful for people managing the side effects of chemotherapy. Ginger is a natural decongestant and antihistamine, and its ability to warm the body and thereby ward off the chills makes it an especially good treatment for common head colds. Ginger contains potent anti-inflammatory compounds called *gingerols* that may help diminish pain in arthritis sufferers and inhibit the occurrence of colon cancer. It's also a fantastic remedy for hay fever sufferers.

GREEN PEAS

Tell your man that one cup of green peas has more protein than a large egg! This may make him eat more of this low-fat member of the bean family. The cancer-fighting compound in green peas is called chlorophyllin, the pigment responsible for giving them and other veggies their shiny green color. This pigment attaches to carcinogens and helps prevent them from being absorbed. Peas also contain an abundance of disease-fighting vitamins C, B, A, niacin, phosphorus, iron, and folate. Folate is reputed to be so important for cardiovascular function that a major 1995 study concluded that 400 micrograms per day could prevent 28,000 cardiovascular deaths per year in the United States. Peas are also an excellent source of soluble fiber, which can lower cholesterol and triglycerides, and they provide nutrients like vitamin K that are important for maintaining bone health.

GREEN TEA

Studies have found that green tea is a healthier choice than almost any beverage, including pure water, because it not only hydrates as well as water, but it also provides a rich supply of antioxidant protection. Green tea contains phenolic compounds that may reduce the risk of cardiovascular disease and stroke and that may help neutralize harmful free radicals. Research has demonstrated that green tea can help decrease blood pressure, stimulate the metabolism, and prevent cancer. One of the main ingredients in green tea is catechin, particularly epigallocatechin gallate (EGCG). EGCG is a powerful anti-oxidant that has been found to lower "bad" LDL cholesterol levels, inhibit the formation of blood clots, cut the incidence of cancer by more than 50 percent (if consumed in sufficient quantities), and even freshen breath! Green tea speeds recovery after a heart attack, and it also appears to speed up the recovery of heart cells.

OATS AND OAT BRAN

Oats are the rising star of the healthy heart. They mop up cholesterol (especially "bad" LDL cholesterol), help lower blood sugar, improve insulin sensitivity, control the appetite, and reduce the risk of heart disease, diabetes, and cancer. Oats contain antioxidants and an abundance of fiber, which keeps you full longer and helps in weight control. Oat bran is the outer layer of the oat kernel; it's rich in soluble fiber called beta-glucan and contains even fewer calories and more fiber than the oat kernel. Oats were the first whole grain to be recognized by the FDA for their cholesterol-lowering properties. When eaten regularly, oat bran has been shown to lower total cholesterol by twenty-five points or more within three short months! Other studies suggest that oat consumption may reduce blood pressure. Oats have been known for centuries as "the power grain" that increases strength and vigor, including erectile function and sex drive.

ONIONS

Onions have been called the "roots of good health" for centuries. Like garlic, they're part of the Allium family; they are rich in the flavonoid quercetin, which can help prevent platelets in the blood from sticking together and forming harmful clots. The same strong sulfur compounds that cause you to tear-up

while cutting onions can help raise "good" HDL cholesterol and lower the "bad" LDL cholesterol. It can also lower triglycerides and blood pressure, decrease the risk of stomach and colon cancer, reduce inflammation, and relieve congestion for asthma sufferers. Consumption of onions as frequently as two or more times per week is associated with a significantly reduced risk of developing colon cancer. The amount of carcinogens produced when meat is cooked using high heat methods decreases when the meat is cooked with onions as well. And on a more day-to-day level, onions can be used as a remedy for flatulence and constipation!

POMEGRANATE JUICE

Pomegranate juice is one of the most talked about health foods of recent years. Pomegranates are rich in tannins, anthocyanins, polyphenols, and vitamin C, all of which are powerful antioxidants that help destroy the free radicals that cause aging and can lead to cancer and heart disease. The antioxidant power of pomegranates is touted to be even greater than that of red wine and green tea. Pomegranate juice works as a blood thinner, reducing plaque in the arteries, raising good cholesterol, and possibly even lowering blood pressure. Promising research indicates that pomegranate juice may also offer significant protection against prostate cancer, as well as managing erectile dysfunction.

SARDINES

These little fish truly contain health and nutrition from the sea. Two sardines have six grams of protein but only fifty calories, so athletes love them. Sardines also contain omega-3 fatty acids, which are known to promote better health by helping to keep arteries open and the heart working well. They can help reduce the risk of heart disease by lowering cholesterol and triglycerides, protect against breast and colon cancers, and reduce lung inflammation in smokers. A recent Japanese study showed a diet that includes fish can help prevent hardening of the arteries in middle-aged men. Eating sardines can also protect against cancer by reducing the body's production of prostaglandins, which are tumor promoters when they occur in large amounts. Eating sardines could also help improve breathing difficulties caused by smoking.

SPINACH

Spinach can help control blood pressure, reduce the risk of heart disease and cancer, and protect against vision loss. It delivers more nutrients for fewer calories than almost any other food; it's loaded with calcium, magnesium, folate, vitamin K, and iron, as well as all the phytochemicals, which helps control cancer, especially colon, lung, and breast. Folate reduces the amount of homocysteine, a protein that damages arteries, in the bloodstream; in turn, spinach helps protect against heart disease. In fact, spinach is probably the best leafy green for managing homocysteine levels. The flavonoids in spinach are touted to help protect against age-related memory loss. Spinach's secret weapons, lutein and zeaxanthin, make it among the best foods for preventing cataracts and age-related macular degeneration, the primary cause of vision loss in older adults. It is also very high in alpha- and beta-carotene, the bodyguards against cancer-causing agents like air pollution, noxious chemicals, and tobacco smoke.

STRAWBERRIES

One of the world's healthiest foods, strawberries are the most popular berry fruit.

They are a dieter's dream, rich in taste and nutrients but low in calories. They are chock-full of pectin, a fiber that reduces cholesterol and helps prevent constipation. They are also rich in ellagic acid, a phytochemical that has been shown to the cancer-causing chemicals in free radicals and cigarette smoke. They are very high in Vitamin C, which prevents cataracts and helps to reduce the risk of heart disease and infection. The phenols found in strawberries have anti-inflammatory properties useful in controlling arthritis, asthma, atherosclerosis (hardening of the arteries), and cancer. For the most nutritious benefits, buy the brightest red berries with their green caps on, wash them, and cut them right before you eat them.

ZUCCHINI

Summer squash in all its varieties shows anti-cancer effects and supports men's health by reducing the symptoms of a condition called benign prostate hypertrophy (BPH), an enlarged prostate that can cause difficulty with urinary and sexual function. With elevated levels of vitamins C and A, fiber, potassium, folate, copper, magnesium, phosphorus, and carotenoids like beta-carotene, zucchini in particular has proven to be helpful in preventing atherosclerosis, the oxidation of cholesterol, and diabetic heart disease. It is also helpful in conditions like asthma and arthritis. Zucchini's content of magnesium and potassium, is helpful for reducing high blood pressure. Their delicate flavor and creamy white flesh make them an ideal choice for Sneaky Chefs.

SWEET POTATOES AND YAMS

Sweet potatoes and yams are packed with vitamins C and E, beta-carotene, calcium, potassium, iron, and dietary fiber. They have been dubbed the "anti-diabetic" food because they stabilize blood sugar levels, prevent blood sugar "spikes and crashes," and lower insulin resistance. Unrelated to the white potato, they are a sweetly nutritious and filling package of protection. They contain the B vitamins folate and B6, which are both believed helpful in preserving brain function. Rich in complex carbs but low in calories, this high-fiber "good" carb is the ultimate comfort food; it actually causes the brain to produce more serotonin (the hormone that relaxes us). When hidden in Sneaky Chef tomato sauce, sweet potatoes add a subtle sweetness and work doubly hard to cut acidity, thereby preventing indigestion.

TOFU

Recent research on soy protein has shown it can help lower total cholesterol levels by as much as 30 percent, lower "bad" LDL cholesterol levels by as much as 35 to 40 percent, lower triglyceride levels, raise levels of "good" HDL cholesterol, and possibly reduce the formation of blood clots. The isoflavones in soy are believed to play a role in it's cholesterol-lowering effects. Tofu is high in protein, calcium, and iron. Most of the fat in tofu is the non-artery-clogging unsaturated kind. And like fish oil, tofu is a good source of omega-3 fatty acids, which also contribute to its heart-protecting benefits. Tofu soaks up the flavor of whatever you put on it, so it's a healthy, highly versatile substitute that can be made to suit any taste.

TOMATOES

Tomatoes may be the single most important food for men's health, and perhaps the easiest to add to the diet on a daily basis. That's because processed tomato products, such as tomato paste, spaghetti sauce, and even ketchup are six times more potent than raw tomatoes in the celebrated antioxidant, lycopene. Lycopene, the nutrient that makes tomatoes red, has been extensively studied and proven to halve the risk of prostate, colon, and stomach cancers and heart attacks, especially when eaten in combination with a little good fat like olive oil, avocado, or nuts, which help the body break it down and absorb it. Organic tomato-based products, such as organic ketchup, have been shown to deliver up to three times the amount of lycopene as non-organic. If for some reason your guy doesn't like tomato products, lycopene is also concentrated in other red-hued fruits such as guava, apricots, watermelon, papaya, and pink grapefruit. Raw tomatoes are also loaded with vitamins A and C, potassium, iron, and fiber.

WALNUTS

Walnuts are among the superstars of the nut family and one of the best plant sources of protein (and we know our guys love their protein!). Studies show that you can lower your risk of cardiovascular disease by as much as 50 percent by eating a handful (about fourteen halves) of unsalted walnuts about five times a week. They are unique as a nutrient-dense whole food source of alpha linolenic acid (ALA), an essential omega-3 fatty acid. Studies are exploring the benefits of walnuts in relation to diabetes and weight management, Parkinson's and Alzheimer's diseases, bone health, and prostate and other cancers. Walnuts also contain the amino acid arginine, a compound that helps expand the blood vessels and keeps platelets from clumping. The high vitamin E content in walnuts keeps "bad" LDL cholesterol from oxidizing, and the generous amounts of heart-healthy magnesium and copper appear to regulate cholesterol, blood pressure, and heart rhythms. Walnuts also contain a good amount of the antioxidant ellagic acid, which is believed to battle cancer on several fronts; it disables free radicals, detoxifies potential cancer-causing substances, and helps prevent cancer cells from dividing.

WHEAT GERM

Nutritionists say there are more nutrients in an ounce of wheat germ than in any other grain product or vegetable! And for guys who love their protein, this food packs 27 grams of it in just 3.5 ounces, giving wheat germ more protein per ounce than most meats! Wheat germ is also an excellent source of zinc, which is important for male fertility; vitamin E and fiber, which aid in digestion and reduce the risk of colon cancer; and iron, B vitamins, folate, and potassium. Wheat germ is one of the few sources of plant-derived omega-3 fatty acids. Wheat germ is beneficial to athletic training and may help increase endurance and cardiovascular function during an intensive training program.

WHITE BEANS AND CHICKPEAS (GARBANZO BEANS)

Small but mighty, these fiber-rich legumes can help lower "bad" LDL cholesterol and raise "good" HDL cholesterol, stabilize blood sugar levels, reduce the risk of breast and prostate cancers, and prevent heart disease in people with diabetes. When added to high-carb/high-sugar foods, beans help stabilize blood-sugar levels, providing steady, slow-burning energy so the guys will feel satisfied longer and have less "brain fog." All beans are excellent sources of folate, tryptophan, magnesium, and iron, providing energy to boost the brain and protect against heart disease and cancer. Beans are the ultimate power food: low in fat, high in protein, fiber, vitamins, and minerals. Chickpeas especially can increase energy by helping to replenish iron stores. They are so filling they help curb your appetite, they are some of the best cancer-fighting foods, and they are referred to as the healthy man's meat. Combined with grains or rice, beans form a whole protein comparable to meat and dairy, and combining beans with foods high in vitamin C will enhance iron absorption. The creamy white color and very mild flavor of white beans make them excellent sneaky ingredients in many recipes.

YOGURT

Yogurt is a fermented dairy product that can boost immunity (especially against pneumonia), lower bad cholesterol, and help heal and prevent ulcers. Every spoonful comes with live organisms and friendly bacteria called probiotics that can provide dramatic improvements in your health, especially in the digestive system. Yogurt is a super source of calcium that dramatically raises *gamma interferon*, a protein that helps the immune system's white blood cells fight disease.

Gamma interferon is the best mechanism the body has to defend itself against salmonella and bacteria-caused ulcers. The friendly bacteria in yogurt also take up residence in the digestive tract and compete with the harmful bacteria that cause ulcers, increasing the efficacy of ulcer medications. Yogurt is an easy-to-digest alternative to low-fat milk, as the live bacteria help break down lactose for lactose-intolerant people. It's also a good source of vitamin D, which boosts the immune system, strengthens bones and teeth, helps prevent colon cancer, and may improve a man's fertility. Yogurt also has been shown to aid in fat loss and retention of lean muscle in weight-loss programs.

CHAPTER SIX

The Recipes

The collection of recipes that follows is the result of an extensive investigation. My team and I interviewed firemen across the nation to learn more about which foods real men love to eat. My brave new friends were kind enough to serve me dinner when I visited their firehouses for the interviews, often their own delicious version of meatloaf and mashed potatoes, with each variation more tasty than the next. Yet these guys were more than happy to allow me to upgrade the nutrition of their favorite meals, so long as I promised that the taste would remain as good as ever.

As I've said many times, I'm not a magi-cian, but the recipes in this book do have the illusion of looking and tasting very similar to their evil twins. They seem decadent, forbidden, and oh so satisfying. No one wants to feel deprived, even in the name of good health, and with my Sneaky Chef recipes, you don't have to. You and your man really can have your cake and eat it, too, with the knowledge that the great-tasting food you're eating is also packed with hidden health benefits. So here are Sloppy Joes for the average Joe—macho meals that men can sink their teeth into and then leave the table feeling satisfied. But these manly meals have been subtly transformed from artery-clogging and gut-busting to artery-*cleansing* and gut-*slimming*. All are as low in fat and sugar as possible, and all are designed to incorporate the latest superfoods—whole grains, legumes, vegetables, nuts, and fruits—scientifically proven to address the most common threats to men's health, such as heart disease, type 2 diabetes, high blood pressure, and even bad moods (which can feel like a disease, even if they're not technically!). And yet when your guy sits down to a bowl of your newly revamped chili and cornbread, all he'll feel is glad to have come home for dinner.

By the way, if anyone wants to cook these foods for their local firehouse, I can attest to the fact that you'll be welcomed and your healthy meal will be appreciated.

JUST A FEW NOTES BEFORE WE BEGIN:

1. The "optional extra boost" at the bottom of some recipes is an undisguised ingredient that is not meant to be hidden. It's mentioned as an option because it adds extra nutrition and some men won't mind eating it. But since the ingredient is visible, you might want to check with your guy before adding it if you don't want to run the risk of having the entire dish discarded. If he really objects, don't add it.

2. The sneaky ingredients in each recipe are highlighted in grey (some people choose the recipe based on these ingredients).

3. As sneaky as my hidden ingredients are, they can be detected if you use too much all at once. I suggest using a small amount of the booster for the first few times you serve a recipe. Gradually increase the amount you include over time, adding as much as you can get away with. If you go too far, just scale back and try again. This way men become acclimated to the subtle flavor differences the Make-Aheads might cause.

4. All of the puree recipe instructions call for a food processor. I have recommended my personal favorite the Kitchen Aid 3-cup Chef's Chopper® Series mini-processor (available on my website www.TheSneakyChef.com) to so many people and with much success. I recommend this handy tool for five good reasons. One, it's amazingly inexpensive, given how useful it is for so many kitchen jobs. Two, it's so small you can leave it on

the countertop so you won't have to go rooting for it in the back of a cupboard. Three, it works well with the relatively small amounts of ingredients in these recipes. Four, it's easier to operate than a large processor. And five, there are fewer parts to wash, so clean-up is simple. However, you can certainly make every recipe in this book with a large food processor or a blender. Just note that larger processors work better with larger amounts of ingredients, so consider doubling the recipes. And the secret to the blender is to put the liquid in first, and to use a little more than is called for. Also, stop frequently so you can push the ingredients to the bottom.

5. Many recipes in this book call for salt. Although I did not specify which type of salt in each recipe, I highly suggest that you use a natural, crystal salt that contains the complete spectrum of minerals your body can absorb. Common table salt is highly processed (like white bread) and stripped of its natural mineral elements. Spending a little more money on a really good salt is one of the easiest ways to improve your family's health.

I recommend Original Himalayan Crystal Salt (available on my website), which is even healthier than the sea salt that's sold in natural food stores. Of course, if you are concerned about health issues that involve salt intake, feel free to cut back on it in all the recipes in this book (except the baked goods).

6. For all recipes calling for eggs or egg whites, feel free to substitute the equivalent amount of Egg Beaters®.

7. Many recipes call for pomegranate juice; I recommend 100 percent pure pomegranate juice without added juices or sweeteners.

8. Readers familiar with my first book, The Sneaky Chef, may recall that I suggested grinding oats in a food processor in some recipes. In this book, I've simplified that process by calling for oat bran, which can be purchased almost anywhere that packaged hot cereals are sold.

9. I often refer to cooking spray oil in the recipes. Use an additive-free, natural olive oil or canola oil spray or mist, or make your own cooking spray by putting the healthy oil of your choice into a spray bottle.

10. You can substitute *fat-free ricotta cheese* wherever part-skim ricotta cheese is called for in a recipe.

11. You'll notice icons at the top of each recipe. They indicate nutrition highlights of each recipe, and a quick way to tell if the recipe fits into your goals:

 Whole Grains: includes a healthy amount of whole grains

 Veggie: vegetarian recipe (may include eggs and dairy, but no fish, poultry, or meat)

 Indulge: has a higher fat and/or sugar content

 Antioxidant Boost: contains a number of antioxidants

 Protein Boost: contains a good amount of protein

 **Low Carb:** contains minimal carbohydrates; ideal for low-carb diets

 Low Sugar: contains no added sugar or sweeteners

 Omega 3s: contains a healthy amount of omega-3 fatty acids

 Healthy Fats: contains heart healthy (monounsaturated) fats, like olive or nut oils, avocado, or nuts

Okay. Now you're ready to take a whole new approach to cooking for yourself and the man in your life by adding nature's super-foods to all his favorite recipes. Like you, I am a busy woman, and I understand how important it is to prepare meals that are quick and easy in addition to being delicious and healthy. Those are the dual aims of this book. So roll up your sleeves and get ready to cheat on your man in the kitchen!

BREAKFAST RECIPES

Legal Donuts

It'll take a top-ranking detective to identify the healthy ingredients in this seemingly sinful breakfast favorite.

MAKES 12 DONUTS OR 6 LARGE MUFFINS

1 cup plus 3 tablespoons Flour Blend (see Make-Ahead Recipe #13)

2 teaspoons baking powder

½ teaspoon salt

1 teaspoon instant coffee granules

½ teaspoon cinnamon

3 tablespoons unsweetened cocoa powder

1 large egg

½ cup sugar

3 tablespoons walnut, almond, or canola oil

¾ cup Purple Puree (see Make-Ahead Recipe #1)

1 teaspoon pure vanilla extract

Powdered sugar, for dusting

Preheat the oven to 350 degrees. If you are making donuts, spray a donut pan or a mini Bundt pan with oil (they come in 6- or 12-mold sizes—use two 6-mold pans if you don't have the 12-mold size). If you are making muffins, line a muffin tin with paper liners.

In a large bowl, whisk together the Flour Blend, baking powder, salt, coffee granules, cinnamon, and cocoa powder. In another large bowl, whisk together the egg and sugar until well combined, then whisk in the oil, Purple Puree, and vanilla. Fold the wet ingredients into the dry and mix until the flour is just moistened. Don't overmix.

Divide the batter evenly among the 12 mini Bundt or donut molds or fill 6 muffin cups to the top.

For donuts: Bake 12 to 14 minutes, until the tops spring back when pressed lightly. Loosen the edges with a knife and turn the donuts out over a plate to cool. Dust with powdered sugar before serving.

For muffins: Bake 23 to 25 minutes, until a toothpick inserted in the center comes out clean. Turn the muffins out of the tins to cool. Dust tops with powdered sugar before serving.

"Never work before breakfast; if you have to work before breakfast, eat your breakfast first."

—*Josh Billings*

Power Breakfast Cookies

anti oxident boost · omega 3s · veggie · whole grains · healthy fats

This great grab-and-go breakfast cookie provides a nice kick-start in the morning with a bit of caffeine from the cocoa and coffee (you can use decaf if you prefer). The teaspoon of sugar in each cookie is less than the average amount in a morning cup of Joe, and the cinnamon, walnuts, and Purple Puree will help hold off hunger longer than most breakfast cereals.

Make a few batches and store extra cookies in plastic bags in your freezer. They defrost quickly on the counter or in the car on the way to work (but they're great frozen, too!).

MAKES 18 COOKIES

1 large egg

6 tablespoons walnut, almond, or canola oil

6 tablespoons brown sugar

1 teaspoon pure vanilla extract

$\frac{3}{4}$ cup Purple Puree (see Make-Ahead Recipe #1)

$1\frac{1}{4}$ cup Flour Blend (see Make-Ahead Recipe #13)

$\frac{1}{2}$ teaspoon baking soda

$\frac{1}{2}$ teaspoon salt

$\frac{1}{4}$ cup unsweetened cocoa powder

2 tablespoons Ground Walnuts (see Make-Ahead Recipe #15)

1 teaspoon cinnamon

2 teaspoons instant coffee granules

Powdered sugar, for dusting

Preheat the oven to 350 degrees. Line a baking sheet with parchment paper (or spray with oil).

In a large bowl, whisk together the egg, oil, brown sugar, vanilla, and Purple Puree. In another large bowl, whisk together the Flour Blend, baking soda, salt, cocoa powder, ground walnuts, cinnamon, and coffee granules. Add the dry ingredients to the wet and mix just enough to moisten the dry ingredients. Drop large tablespoonfuls of batter onto the baking sheets, leaving about an inch between each cookie. Flatten the cookies with the back of a fork. Bake 12 to 14 minutes, until lightly browned around the edges.

Remove from the pan and let cool on a rack. Dust with a little powdered sugar and serve with Sinless Smoothies, page 166, or Sneak-a-Chinos, page 162.

Cinnamon Toast Breakfast Biscotti

anti oxident boost   omega 3s   veggie   whole grains   protein boost

Once I discovered how easy it is to bake biscotti—which are simply twice-baked cookie slices—a whole new world opened up to me. I make these on the weekend and we have a portable breakfast all week long. They have more protein and fiber and less fat than breakfast at the fitness club. Store them in an airtight container for up to 3 days, or freeze them in a plastic bag for up to 3 months. Enjoy them on the train to work—as long as your seatmates don't mind the crunch!

MAKES 16 BISCOTTI

2 cups high-fiber cereal flakes

2 tablespoons Ground Walnuts
(see Make-Ahead Recipe #15)

1 teaspoon baking powder

1 teaspoon cinnamon

$\frac{1}{2}$ teaspoon salt

$\frac{3}{4}$ cup Flour Blend (see Make-Ahead
Recipe #13)

$\frac{2}{3}$ cup part-skim ricotta cheese

1 large egg

2 tablespoons walnut, almond, or canola oil

$\frac{1}{3}$ cup brown sugar

1 teaspoon pure vanilla extract

Cinnamon sugar, for dusting

Optional extra boost: 1 cup dried cranberries
or dried blueberries

Preheat the oven to 350 degrees. Line a baking sheet with parchment paper (or spray with oil).

Using a rolling pin, gently crush the cereal (in a sealed plastic bag) into coarsely crushed flakes. Alternatively, pulse the cereal in a food processor.

In a large bowl, whisk together the ground walnuts, baking powder, cinnamon, salt, Flour Blend, and crushed cereal. In another large bowl, whisk together the ricotta, egg, oil, brown sugar, and vanilla. Add the dry ingredients to the wet and mix just enough to moisten the dry ingredients. Stir in the cranberries or blueberries, if using.

Place the dough on the prepared baking sheet and use your fingers to form it into a log approximately 4 inches wide x 9 inches long. Bake for 20 minutes, remove from the oven, and let cool for 5 minutes.

Place the log on a cutting board. Using a serrated knife, cut the log into diagonal slices about ½-inch thick. Place the slices back on the baking sheet, sprinkle them with cinnamon sugar, and bake for another 15 minutes. Flip the biscotti over, sprinkle the other side with cinnamon sugar, and bake for a final 15 minutes, until nicely browned.

Serve with coffee or tea, for dipping.

Chocolate-Charged French Toast

With its antioxidant properties, cocoa is a powerful booster ingredient on its own, but in this recipe it also camouflages the dark color of whole grain bread and the Purple Puree in the batter, allowing you to sneak in even more beneficial ingredients. For quicker French toast in the morning, you can make this batter the night before and leave it covered in the refrigerator overnight. Don't forget to dust with a little powdered sugar before serving for extra visual appeal.

MAKES 6 SLICES OF FRENCH TOAST

4 egg whites

$\frac{1}{4}$ cup Purple Puree (see Make-Ahead Recipe #1)

1 teaspoon pure vanilla extract

1 tablespoon pure maple syrup

2 teaspoons unsweetened cocoa powder

$\frac{1}{4}$ teaspoon salt

6 slices whole grain bread

Nonstick cooking spray (for greasing skillet)

6 teaspoons semisweet chocolate chips

Powdered sugar, for dusting

In a large shallow baking dish, whisk together the egg whites, Purple Puree, vanilla, maple syrup, cocoa powder, and salt.

Generously spray a large skillet with oil. Dip each slice of bread in the egg mixture until it's soaked through, then flip and soak the other side. Cook for about 3 minutes per side (flip when lightly browned on one side). To serve, place 1 teaspoon of chocolate chips between two slices of stacked French toast and dust lightly with powdered sugar.

Top Banana Waffles

(anti oxident boost) (omega 3s) (veggie) (whole grains)

These waffles look and taste decadent, but when you make them for your sweetie on Sunday morning, you'll have done your good deed for the day. The healthy combination of sweet potatoes, carrots, walnuts, and bananas will satisfy any hungry man—especially a man who doesn't want to feel like he's on a diet!

MAKES 4 WAFFLES

4 egg whites

1 teaspoon pure vanilla extract

¼ teaspoon salt

½ cup Orange Puree (see Make-Ahead Recipe #2)

2 teaspoons maple syrup, plus additional for serving

2 large bananas, mashed with the back of a fork (about ½ cup)

2 tablespoons Ground Walnuts (see Make-Ahead Recipe #15)

¾ cup Flour Blend (see Make-Ahead Recipe #13)

2 teaspoons baking powder

½ teaspoon cinnamon

Milk, as needed

Preheat a waffle iron to medium-high and spray with oil.

In a large mixing bowl, whisk together the egg whites, vanilla, salt, Orange Puree, maple syrup, mashed bananas, and ground walnuts. In a large bowl, whisk together the Flour Blend, baking powder, and cinnamon. Add the wet ingredients to the dry, stirring until just blended. Batter should be fairly thick and slightly lumpy. But if too thick, add a touch of milk.

Spoon ⅓ to ½ cup batter onto the center of the prepared waffle iron (the amount of batter needed will vary according to the size and type of the waffle iron you're using). Close the top and cook until the waffle is lightly browned, crisp, and lifts easily off the grids, about 5 minutes. Repeat with the remaining batter, spraying the waffle iron with more oil if needed.

Serve immediately as the waffles come off the iron, or keep them warm on a plate, covered with aluminum foil. Serve drizzled with maple syrup.

Sneaky Tip:

To make your morning breakfast quicker, you can make the batter for any of the sneaky pancake and waffle recipes the night before and leave it covered in the refrigerator overnight.

Wiley Walnut Waffles

If you can't get your man to sit down to a bowl of oats and low-fat yogurt, these waffles offer the same health benefits in a sneaky package. The optional chocolate chips act as the only sweetener in this recipe. Alternatively, serve with a drizzle of maple syrup.

MAKES 4 WAFFLES

4 egg whites

1 teaspoon pure vanilla extract

$\frac{1}{4}$ teaspoon salt

$\frac{1}{2}$ cup low-fat yogurt, plain or vanilla

$\frac{1}{4}$ cup low-fat or skim milk

$\frac{1}{4}$ cup Ground Walnuts (see Make-Ahead Recipe #15)

$\frac{1}{2}$ cup oat bran

2 teaspoons baking powder

$\frac{1}{3}$ cup Flour Blend (see Make-Ahead Recipe #13)

$\frac{1}{4}$ cup semisweet chocolate chips, or $\frac{1}{2}$ cup fresh or frozen (not thawed) blueberries, (optional)

Preheat the waffle iron to medium-high and spray with oil.

In a medium bowl, whisk together the egg whites, vanilla, salt, yogurt, milk, and ground walnuts. In another large bowl, whisk together the oat bran, baking powder, and Flour Blend. Stir the wet ingredients into the dry ingredients until just blended. Mix in the chocolate chips or blueberries, if using. If batter is too thick, add a touch more milk.

Serve immediately as the waffles come off the iron, or keep them warm on a plate, covered with aluminum foil.

Blockbuster Blueberry Muffins

anti oxident boost · veggie · whole grains

These days, the average supersized muffin costs you half a day's calories and fat grams. The ones that taste good are no better than cupcakes without the icing (and the ones that are whole grain and low-fat taste just like the box they came in!). If you want the best of both worlds—great taste and lower fat—these muffins may become your family's favorite morning staple. White Bean Puree works overtime to cut the fat and provide fiber, and the oat bran and wheat germ disappear behind the world's healthiest berry.

Be sure to make extras and freeze them in a plastic bag. When you're ready to eat, simply pull one out and toast it!

MAKES 6 LARGE MUFFINS

2 large eggs

¼ cup sugar

¼ cup almond or canola oil

½ cup White Bean Puree (see Make-Ahead Recipe #9)

2 teaspoons pure vanilla extract

¾ cup Flour Blend (see Make-Ahead Recipe #13)

2 teaspoons baking powder

½ teaspoon cinnamon

½ cup oat bran

½ teaspoon salt

1 cup fresh or frozen (not thawed) blueberries

Preheat the oven to 375 degrees. Line a muffin tin with paper liners.

In a large bowl, whisk together the eggs and sugar until well combined, then whisk in the oil, White Bean Puree, and vanilla. In another bowl, whisk together the Flour Blend, baking powder, cinnamon, oat bran, and salt. Fold the dry ingredients into the wet, mixing until the flour is just moistened, then lightly mix in the blueberries. Don't overmix, or the muffins will be dense.

Fill each muffin cup to the top, spooning about $\frac{1}{4}$ cup of batter into each. Bake for 22 to 25 minutes, until the tops are golden brown.

Grilled Muffin Variation

Once cool, slice the muffins in half, butter each side very lightly, and place buttered-side down on a hot indoor grill pan or outdoor grill until toasted the muffin is toasted and grill marks appear. Serve hot, with coffee.

Blueberry Crumb Variation

Follow the instructions for Blockbuster Blueberry Muffins, but add one tablespoon of Feel Good Fruit Crisp Topping, page 328, to the top of each muffin before baking.

"Be careful about reading health books. You may die of a misprint."

—Mark Twain

Bonanza Crunch Muffins

I used these muffins as an intro to one of my cooking-school classes; my students devoured them as I discussed the theory behind the Sneaky Chef method. In this case, a taste was worth a thousand words—I asked them take the "Sneaky Chef Challenge," and there wasn't a single person who could identify the hidden sweet potatoes or carrots inside. As with all sneaky muffins, these freeze well. Just pop them in the toaster to warm up.

MAKES 6 LARGE MUFFINS

1 large egg

¼ cup sugar

¼ cup almond or canola oil

6 tablespoons Orange Puree (see Make-Ahead Recipe #2)

2 large bananas, mashed with the back of a fork (about ½ cup)

1 teaspoon pure vanilla extract

¾ cup Flour Blend (see Make-Ahead Recipe #13)

2 teaspoons baking powder

½ teaspoon cinnamon

½ cup oat bran

½ teaspoon salt

¼ cup chopped walnuts, for topping (optional)

Preheat the oven to 375 degrees. Line a muffin tin with paper liners.

In a large bowl, whisk together the egg and sugar until well combined, then whisk in the oil, Orange Puree, bananas, and vanilla. In another bowl, whisk together the Flour Blend, baking powder, cinnamon, oat bran, and salt. Fold the dry ingredients into the wet, and mix until the flour is just moistened. Don't overmix, or the muffins will be dense.

Fill each muffin cup to the top, spooning about ¼ cup of batter into each. Sprinkle the tops with a few chopped walnuts, if using, and bake for 24 to 26 minutes, until the tops are golden brown.

Grilled Muffin Variation

Once cool, slice the muffins in half, butter each side very lightly, and place buttered-side down on a hot indoor grill pan or outdoor grill until the muffin is toasted and grill marks appear. Serve hot, with coffee.

Sneak-a-Chinos

Trendy coffee milkshakes have inched their way up to a whopping 600+ calories and 25+ grams of fat —about the equivalent of a double cheeseburger. If you want the creamy, frozen satisfaction without the fattening consequences, try these sneak-a-chinos. Not only are they less sinful, they also sport some super healthy ingredients like spinach, avocado, and blueberries lurking under the whipped cream!

Mocha Flavor

anti oxident boost · omega 3s · veggie · healthy fats

½ cup strong coffee (with or without caffeine)

¼ cup low-fat or skim milk

¼ ripe avocado

2 teaspoons unsweetened cocoa powder, plus additional for garnish

1 tablespoon semisweet chocolate chips

1 to 2 teaspoons sugar

1 cup ice

Whipped cream, for garnish

Blend all ingredients except garnishes together in a blender until smooth. Serve in a tall glass with a quick squirt of whipped cream, a light dusting of cocoa powder, and a straw.

Blueberry Flavor

anti oxident boost veggie

¼ cup strong coffee (with or without caffeine)

¼ cup low-fat or skim milk

¼ cup Purple Puree (see Make-Ahead Recipe #1)

1 to 2 teaspoons sugar

1 cup ice

Whipped cream, for garnish

Cocoa powder, for garnish

Blend all ingredients except garnishes together in a blender until smooth. Serve in a tall glass with a quick squirt of whipped cream, a light dusting of cocoa powder, and a straw.

SIX SIMPLE "S" STRATEGIES FOR STAYING SLIM

1. SIT DOWN when you eat anything

2. SOUP OR SALAD to start the meal

3. SLOW DOWN by putting your fork down between bites

4. SEE if a craving will pass by waiting 10 minutes before indulging

5. SAY "YES" to an indulgence once in a while

6. SIP eight ounces of room-temperature water fifteen minutes before each meal

Stacked Pancakes

Breakfast at the health spa never tasted like this. These pancakes have more nutrition than a boring bowl of oatmeal, but they have the look and taste of a white flour pancake (and yet there is absolutely no flour in them!) and enough protein and whole grains to keep your man energized all morning long.

If your mornings are rushed (and whose aren't?!), make the batter the night before, then serve freshly made pancakes any day of the week; or place the cooked pancakes in a plastic bag and freeze them for months, then simply toast them in the morning. These pancakes also hold up well as a "grab and go" handheld breakfast in the car on the way to work.

MAKES 8 TO 10 LARGE PANCAKES

4 egg whites

$\frac{1}{2}$ cup part-skim or fat-free ricotta cheese

1 teaspoon pure vanilla extract

1 teaspoon baking powder

$\frac{1}{4}$ teaspoon salt

$\frac{1}{2}$ cup oat bran

$\frac{1}{4}$ cup Ground Almonds (see Make-Ahead Recipe #14)

$\frac{1}{4}$ cup semisweet chocolate chips or $\frac{1}{2}$ cup fresh or frozen (not thawed) blueberries (optional)

Maple syrup, warmed, for serving

In a large bowl, whisk together the egg whites, ricotta, and vanilla. In another large bowl, whisk together the baking powder, salt, oat bran, and ground almonds. Stir the wet ingredients into the dry until just blended. Batter should be fairly thick and slightly lumpy. But if the batter is too thick, add a touch of milk. Add the chocolate chips or blueberries, if using, and mix lightly.

Butter or spray a large skillet over medium heat. Test the pan by tossing in a few drops of water; it will sizzle when it's hot enough. The skillet will grow hotter over time, so turn down the heat if the pan starts to smoke.

Drop medium-size ladles of batter onto the skillet in batches, making sure there are some chocolate chips or blueberries in each pancake. When bubbles begin to set around the edges and the skillet-side of each pancake is golden (peek underneath), gently flip them over. Continue to cook 2 to 3 minutes or until the pancake is fully set.

Serve stacked high, drizzled with a little warm maple syrup.

Cinnamon apple pancake variation

Follow the instructions for Stacked Pancakes, adding ½ teaspoon of cinnamon and substituting a peeled, chopped apple for the chocolate chips or blueberries. For smoother texture, grate the apple before adding it to the batter. Serve with a dusting of cinnamon sugar.

Sinless Smoothies

If your guy isn't a morning person, he may prefer to drink his breakfast rather than chew it. Wake up his taste buds with a cool blend of the world's healthiest superfoods in these delicious smoothies.

EACH VARIATION MAKES 1 TALL SMOOTHIE

Blueberry Smoothie

anti oxident boost · omega 3s · veggie · healthy fats

1 green tea bag

¼ ripe avocado

¼ cup plus 2 tablespoons pomegranate juice

½ cup frozen blueberries (no syrup or sugar added)

1 tablespoon honey or maple syrup

4 to 6 ice cubes

Steep the tea bag in ½ cup boiling water for 2 minutes (no longer or it will taste bitter). Allow the tea to cool.

In the container of a blender, combine ½ cup of tea with the avocado, pomegranate juice, blueberries, honey, and ice cubes and pulse until smooth. Serve in a tall glass with a straw.

Sneaky Tip:

Research published in the International Journal of Impotence Research finds drinking 8 ounces of POM Wonderful 100% Pomegranate Juice daily may help boost blood flow and manage erectile dysfunction and impotence.

Cherry Smoothie

anti oxident boost · omega 3s · veggie · healthy fats

1 green tea bag

¼ ripe avocado

¼ cup plus 2 tablespoons pomegranate juice

½ cup frozen cherries (no syrup or sugar added)

1 tablespoon honey or maple syrup

4 to 6 ice cubes

Steep the tea bag in ½ cup boiling water for 2 minutes (no longer or it will taste bitter). Allow the tea to cool.

In the container of a blender, combine the tea with the avocado, pomegranate juice, cherries, honey, and ice cubes and pulse until smooth. Serve in a tall glass with a straw.

Strawberry Smoothie

anti oxident boost · omega 3s · veggie · healthy fats

1 green tea bag

1 large frozen banana (see Make-Ahead Recipe #11)

1/4 ripe avocado

1/4 cup plus 2 tablespoons pomegranate juice

½ cup frozen strawberries (no syrup or sugar added)

1 tablespoon honey or maple syrup

4 to 6 ice cubes

Steep the tea bag in ½ cup boiling water for 2 minutes (no longer or the tea will taste bitter). Allow to cool.

In the container of a blender, combine the tea with the banana, avocado, pomegranate juice, strawberries, honey, and ice cubes and pulse until smooth. Serve in a tall glass with a straw.

Hobo Hash

anti oxident boost *low sugar* *omega 3s* *veggie* *healthy fats* *protein boost*

When my family skis in Steamboat Springs, Colorado, our favorite breakfast is called a "Hobo" at a local restaurant. It keeps us warm and energized all morning on the slopes. I've managed to improve its nutritional profile while staying true to the taste by hiding White Bean Puree, tofu, and egg whites in the hash.

MAKES 2 SERVINGS

1 tablespoon extra-virgin olive oil

½ small onion, diced (about ½ cup)

½ cup frozen shredded low-fat hash browns, thawed and drained

2 large eggs

2 egg whites

¼ cup salsa, plus additional for serving

2 tablespoons White Bean Puree (see Make-Ahead Recipe #9)

¼ cup (⅛ of a 14-ounce block) extra-firm tofu, diced

¼ cup shredded low-fat cheese (any type)

Salt and freshly ground pepper, to taste

Optional extra boost: 1 green bell pepper, diced

Heat the oil over medium-high heat in a large ovenproof skillet. Add the onion and cook until lightly browned, about 5 minutes. Add the hash browns and bell pepper, if using, and stir to combine. Cook until the potatoes are crisp, about 5 minutes.

Preheat the broiler. In a medium-size bowl, whisk together the eggs, egg whites, salsa, White Bean Puree, and tofu. Pour the egg mixture over the potatoes and onions in the skillet and let it set without stirring it. After about 3 minutes, sprinkle the cheese evenly over the top and put the skillet under the broiler for 2 to 3 minutes, until the cheese is slightly browned. Season with salt and pepper and serve with extra salsa.

Hash Brown Patties

The ultimate Sneaky Chef challenge is revamping a greasy truck stop favorite to make it less of a guilty pleasure and more of a nutrition-packed meal! The answer for this particular favorite turned out to be starting with frozen shredded hash browns with almost no fat, sneaking in my White Bean Puree and oat bran, and oven-frying them with just a mist of olive oil. I challenge any trucker to turn these puppies down!

MAKES 6 PATTIES

1 cup frozen shredded low-fat hash browns, thawed and drained

¼ teaspoon salt

½ teaspoon onion powder

¼ cup White Bean Puree (see Make-Ahead Recipe #9)

¼ cup oat bran

¼ cup shredded low-fat cheddar cheese

Optional extra boost: 1 small onion, grated or pureed

Preheat the oven to 400 degrees. Line a baking sheet with parchment paper (or spray with oil

In a medium-size bowl, mix together the hash browns, salt, onion powder, White Bean Puree, oat bran, cheese, and onion, if using. Form ¼-cup sized scoops of the hash brown mixture into flat patties and place them on the prepared baking sheet. Spray the tops of the patties with oil and bake for 20 minutes. Remove the pan from the oven, flip the patties, spray the other side with oil, and bake for another 20 minutes. Serve as a hot side dish, or let cool and store in a plastic bag in the freezer for use within 3 months (simply toast when ready to eat).

French Toast Bites

anti oxident boost · low sugar · veggie · whole grains · protein boost

When you think of healthy foods, cheese Danishes don't usually come to mind, but these stuffed French toast bites have the familiar taste and feel of a Danish without the gut-stuffing rich ingredients. Let the kids help out with this fun treat for Dad. Mine love to roll out the bread and paint on the secret cheese mixture (they don't have to know you mixed in tofu first!).

MAKES 2 SERVINGS (12 TWO-BITE PIECES)

4 slices whole grain bread
   (cinnamon raisin bread works well)

$\frac{1}{4}$ cup ($\frac{1}{8}$ of a 14-ounce block) firm tofu,
   mashed well or pureed in a food processor

$\frac{1}{4}$ cup part-skim or fat-free ricotta cheese

4 egg whites

$\frac{1}{2}$ teaspoon cinnamon

$\frac{1}{4}$ teaspoon salt

1 teaspoon pure vanilla extract

1 tablespoon canola oil

Cinnamon sugar, for dusting

Use a rolling pin to roll out each slice of bread on a cutting board until flattened. In a small bowl, mix the tofu with the ricotta cheese. Spread about 2 tablespoons of the tofu-ricotta mixture on each flattened slice of bread, keeping about $\frac{1}{4}$ inch away from the edges. Roll up each slice of bread, pressing to seal the edges, and cut each roll into 3 horizontal pieces.

In a large shallow baking dish, whisk together the egg whites, cinnamon, salt, and vanilla. Dip each piece in the egg mixture until saturated on all sides, then cook in a well-greased skillet over moderate heat, turning to brown each side. Remove from heat and lightly dust each piece with cinnamon sugar before serving.

LUNCH PAIL RECIPES

Tricky Tuna Sandwich

anti oxident boost | low sugar | omega 3s | whole grains | healthy fats | protein boost

Big fish meets little fish when you hide sardines in with tuna. Here the little sardines pack in big benefits, adding more calcium and omega-3s without the harmful mercury that comes in the tuna. Start by adding the lesser amount of the secret sardines and increase the quantity each time you make this dish. You can also cut back on potentially harmful mercury by using "chunk light" tuna, which contains one-third the mercury of "chunk white." This recipe works best with one or all of the optional extras for great taste, extra nutrients, and a satisfying crunch.

MAKES 2 SANDWICHES

1 (6-ounce) can "chunk light" tuna, packed in water, drained

2 to 4 ounces skinless and boneless sardines, packed in water, drained

2 teaspoons light mayonnaise

2 teaspoons White Bean Puree (see Make-Ahead Recipe #9)

2 teaspoons oat bran

Salt and freshly ground pepper, to taste

4 slices whole grain bread

Optional extra boost: a handful of capers; chopped fresh dill, celery, and onions; red leaf lettuce leaves.

Combine the tuna, sardines, mayonnaise, White Bean Puree, oat bran, and any of the optional extra boost ingredients you are using. Season with salt and pepper to taste. Make sandwiches on whole grain bread with tuna salad and any optional ingredients.

* Lunch pail food safety note: Keep all perishables in a refrigerator or an insulated cooler bag with ice packs until it's time to eat.

Egg-Me-On Salad Sandwich

anti oxident boost · low sugar · low sugar · veggie · protein boost

If your guy likes thick, old-fashioned egg salad sandwiches, he'll love this recipe. He won't notice the missing egg yolks or the hidden, cholesterol-cutting tofu and White Bean Puree, both of which increase the volume of the salad while reducing the fat.

MAKES 2 SANDWICHES

4 large eggs

1 cup (½ of a 14-ounce block) firm tofu

2 tablespoons light mayonnaise

2 teaspoons mustard

2 tablespoons White Bean Puree (see Make-Ahead Recipe #9)

Salt and freshly ground pepper, to taste

4 slices whole grain bread

Optional extra boost: chopped celery and pickles; lettuce leaves

Place the eggs in a small pot and cover with cold water. Bring the water to a boil over high heat; cover, reduce heat to low, and simmer for 10 minutes. Use a slotted spoon to remove the eggs from the simmering water and place them in a bowl of cold water to cool.

Place the tofu in the simmering water for 2 minutes. Whisk the mayonnaise, mustard, and White Bean Puree in a bowl. Drain the tofu, chop it into small pieces, and add it to the mayonnaise mixture.

Once eggs are cool enough to handle, crack and peel them. Cut the eggs in half lengthwise, remove 2 yolks, and set them aside for another use. Chop the whites and the remaining yolks into small pieces. Add them to the tofu mixture and stir together all ingredients, including any optional extras, until well combined. Season with salt and pepper, and serve on whole grain bread with any optional ingredients.

Chicken Waldorf Wrap

anti oxident boost | low carb | low sugar | omega 3s | whole grains | healthy fats | protein boost

Loaded with superfoods—walnuts, grapes, white beans, apples, and wheat germ—this flavorful chicken salad also has a satisfying crunch. Mix in the Super Bowl of Nuts, page 306, to add a kick of spice and nutrition. For convenience, both the salad and the wrap can be made up to one day ahead if kept refrigerated.

MAKES 2 WRAPS

¼ cup light mayonnaise

2 tablespoons White Bean Puree
   (see Make-Ahead Recipe #9)

4½ teaspoons freshly squeezed lemon juice

2 tablespoons wheat germ

Salt and freshly ground pepper, to taste

½ cup chopped walnuts (or use Super Bowl
   of Nuts, page 306)

1 tart apple (like Granny Smith), chopped
   (about 2 cups)

3 celery ribs, chopped (about 1½ cups)

2 cups grapes (red or green, seedless)

2 cups cubed roasted chicken, ideally
   white meat

2 large whole wheat tortillas

Optional extra boost: romaine lettuce leaves

In a large bowl, whisk together the mayonnaise, White Bean Puree, lemon juice, wheat germ, and salt and pepper. Mix in the walnuts, apple, celery, grapes, and chicken, tossing well to coat evenly.

Spoon about half the mixture of the chicken salad onto the bottom third of each tortilla. Top with lettuce, if using. Fold the bottom quarter of each tortilla up and over the filling, fold both sides toward the middle, and roll into sealed packets. Tightly wrap the packets in parchment paper to secure.

QUICK FIXES FOR CONDIMENTS

Because each ingredient has a different shelf life, don't make these enhanced condiments ahead for future use or store them in the original condiment container.

CONDIMENT	QUICK FIX
Barbecue sauce	2 parts barbecue sauce to 1 part Orange or White Puree
Blue cheese dressing	2 parts blue cheese dressing to 1 part plain yogurt or White Puree
Chipotle in adobo sauce	2 parts adobo sauce to 1 part Orange or White Puree
Cranberry sauce	2 parts cranberry sauce to 1 part Orange Puree
French dressing	2 parts French dressing to 1 part White Puree or Orange Puree
Ketchup	2 parts ketchup to 1 part Orange Puree
Mayonnaise	1 part light mayonnaise to 1 part White Bean Puree
Mustard	2 parts mustard to 1 part White Bean Puree
Peanut butter	2 parts peanut butter to 1 part Orange or White or White Bean Puree
Ranch dressing	3 parts ranch dressing to 1 part White Puree or plain yogurt; 1 part Green Puree (makes Green Goddess)
Red horseradish	2 parts horseradish to 1 part White or Orange Puree
Salsa	2 parts salsa to 1 part White or Orange Puree
Steak sauce	2 parts steak sauce to 1 part White or Orange Puree
Thousand Island dressing	2 parts Thousand Island to 1 part White Puree or Orange Puree

Boosted Buffalo Wings Wrap

anti oxident boost · **indulge** · **low carb** · **low sugar** · **healthy fats** · **protein boost**

With the Boosted Buffalo Wings Wrap, bar food meets the lunch pail, to a beneficial result. This wrap has all the flavor and spice of classic buffalo wings, without the fatty wing skin. With the help of low-fat ricotta and White Puree, even the typically high-fat blue cheese dressing has been converted into a health food. These wraps can be made a day ahead and refrigerated.

MAKES 2 WRAPS

¼ cup Bountiful Blue
  Cheese Dressing,
  page 239

4 celery ribs, chopped
  (about 2 cups)

½ cup cooked, shredded
  chicken breast

Hot sauce, to taste

2 large whole wheat
  tortilla wraps

Optional extra boost:
  romaine lettuce leaves

In a large bowl, mix together the blue cheese dressing, celery, chicken, and hot sauce. Spread half the chicken mixture onto the bottom third of each tortilla. Top with the lettuce leaves, if using. Fold the bottom quarter of each tortilla up and over the filling, fold both sides toward the middle, and roll into sealed packets. Tightly wrap the packets in parchment paper to secure.

PUREES—CLOCKWISE FROM LEFT:

Sneaky Ingredients: Purple Puree (blueberries/spinach), Green Puree (spinach/broccoli/peas),
White Puree (cauliflower/zucchini), Orange Puree (sweet potatoes/carrots)

MIGHTY MASHED POTATOES

Sneaky Ingredients:

Cauliflower

Zucchini

White beans

Yogurt

SNEAKY MAKE-AHEAD INGREDIENTS (FROM LEFT, CLOCKWISE):

Ground Walnuts

Turkey Bacon Bits

Oat Bran

Ground Almonds

BAKED CLAMS

Sneaky Ingredients: Almonds, Cornmeal

COLD SESAME NOODLES

Sneaky Ingredients: Cauliflower, Zucchini

BOOSTED BUFFALO WINGS

Sneaky Ingredients:

Cauliflower

Zucchini

CONCEALED CRAB CAKES

Sneaky Ingredients:

White beans

Wheat germ

DON'T-BE-SORRY CALAMARI

Sneaky Ingredients: Cauliflower, Zucchini, Almonds, Cornmeal

BETTER BATTER ONION RINGS

Sneaky Ingredients: Cauliflower, Zucchini, Almonds, Cornmeal

MEGA MARINARA SAUCE

Sneaky Ingredients: Sweet potatoes, Carrots, Cauliflower, Zucchini

GREEN TEA AND POMEGRANATE MANGARITAS

Sneaky Ingredients: Green tea, Pomegranate

BOWLING NIGHT BOLOGNESE

Sneaky Ingredients:

Spinach

Broccoli

Peas

Oat Bran

STUFFED MANLI-COTTI

Sneaky Ingredients:

Tofu

Cauliflower

Zucchini

DOCTOR'S CHOICE CHILI

Sneaky Ingredients: Spinach, Broccoli, Peas, Cauliflower, Zucchini

Side of Slaw

anti oxident boost   low carb   veggie   whole grains

Need a sneaky side dish for a backyard barbecue or to accompany your man's sandwich at lunch? Guys will gobble this one up, blissfully unaware that they're munching on beans, bran, and tofu in their side of slaw.

MAKES 6 SERVINGS

6 tablespoons White Bean Puree (see Make-Ahead Recipe #9)

6 tablespoons light mayonnaise

1 teaspoon celery seed

¼ cup oat bran

1 tablespoon sugar

Salt and freshly ground pepper, to taste

1 (16-ounce) bag pre-washed cole slaw mix

Optional extra boost:

2 tablespoons toasted slivered almonds; 2 green onions, chopped

In a large serving bowl, whisk together the White Bean Puree, mayonnaise, celery seed, oat bran, sugar, and salt and freshly ground pepper. Add the cole slaw mix and toss well. Garnish with the slivered almonds and green onions, if using. Serve chilled.

Sneaky Tip:

Green onions, also called scallions, have significant prostate cancer–fighting properties. In one study, men who ate as little as one-tenth of an ounce of green onions per day experienced a 70 percent reduction in the risk of developing prostate cancer.

Packed Potato Salad

This is a classic potato salad, perfect for a guy who doesn't like fancier versions. The herbs add great flavor, but feel free to omit them if seeing green will make him see red! If you decide to limit yourself to the healthiest of all the optional extra boosts, go for the green onions.

MAKES 4 SERVINGS

2 pounds small Yukon gold or small white potatoes

½ cup White Bean Puree (see Make-Ahead Recipe #9)

¼ cup light mayonnaise

2 tablespoons freshly squeezed lemon juice

2 teaspoons Dijon mustard

1 teaspoon fresh tarragon and/or fresh dill (optional)

Salt and freshly ground pepper, to taste

Optional extra boost: ½ cup chopped celery and/or red or green onions

Peel the potatoes if you don't want to see the skins in the potato salad, then place them in a large pot of cold, salted water. Bring the water to a boil, lower the heat, and simmer, covered, for 20 to 25 minutes, until the potatoes are just tender. Drain the potatoes in a colander and let cool.

In a bowl large enough to hold the potatoes, whisk together the White Bean Puree, mayonnaise, lemon juice, mustard, fresh herbs, salt and pepper, and celery and/or onions, if using.

When the potatoes are cool enough to handle, quarter them and add them to the bowl, stirring gently until all the potatoes are coated with the mayonnaise mixture. Serve immediately or refrigerate for up to 3 days.

Tailgate Turkey Slaw Wrap

anti oxident boost · low sugar · veggie · whole grains · protein boost

MAKES 2 WRAPS

½ pound deli-sliced
    roasted turkey

2 cups Side of Slaw,
    page 185

2 large whole wheat
    tortillas

Place half of the turkey slices on the bottom half of each tortilla and top each with 1 cup of coleslaw. Fold the bottom quarter of each tortilla up and over the filling, fold both sides toward the middle, and roll into sealed packets. Tightly wrap the packets in parchment paper to secure.

Sneaky Tip:

If your guy sits at a computer all day for work, encourage him to stand up and walk around the office every couple of hours. Sitting keeps your muscles from massaging your veins, decreasing blood flow. According to a study by the Medical Institute of New Zealand, sitting at a desk all day could even cause deep vein thrombosis, or clots in the legs or lungs.

Burly Burrito

MAKES 2 BURRITOS

½ cup Blastin' Bean Dip, page 303

½ cup cooked brown rice

2 large whole wheat tortillas

¼ cup shredded low-fat cheddar cheese

Optional extra boost:

shredded romaine, salsa, chopped black olives, thin onion slices

Spoon about ¼ cup of the bean dip and ¼ cup of brown rice onto the bottom third of each tortilla. Top with 2 tablespoons cheese and any or all of the optional toppings. Fold the bottom quarter of each tortilla up and over the filling, fold both sides toward the middle, and roll into sealed packets. Tightly wrap the packets in parchment paper to secure.

These burritos can be made a day ahead and refrigerated; instruct your man to pop the wrapped burrito in the microwave for 1 minute before eating.

Not-for-Chicks Chicken Salad

(anti oxident boost) (low carb) (low sugar) (omega 3s) (whole grains) (protein boost)

Keep your guy from sneaking out for a fast food lunch with this ultra-satisfying mouthful. The increased fiber from the White Bean Puree not only cuts the mayo's fat, it also helps keep his energy high and appeases his appetite all afternoon. Throw in his favorite crunchy chopped veggies for another nutritional bonus. For convenience, the chicken salad can be made up to a day ahead and stored in the refrigerator.

MAKES 2 SANDWICHES

¼ cup light mayonnaise

2 tablespoons White Bean Puree
(see Make-Ahead Recipe #9)

4½ teaspoons freshly squeezed lemon juice

2 tablespoons wheat germ

Salt and freshly ground pepper, to taste

2 cups (about 12 ounces) cubed roasted
chicken, ideally white meat

Optional extra boost: 2 celery ribs, chopped;
1 small onion, chopped; lettuce and
tomato

4 slices whole grain bread

In a large bowl, whisk together the mayonnaise, White Bean Puree, lemon juice, wheat germ, and salt and pepper. Mix in the chicken and the celery and/or onions, if using. Toss well to coat evenly.

Make each sandwich on whole grain bread with about 1 cup of chicken salad and lettuce and/or tomato, if using.

Revamped Reuben

*On a recent trip back to Rick's hometown of Cleveland, we ate at his family's favorite deli, which is famous for its Reuben sandwich. As my husband ordered this fried monstrosity stuffed with artery-clogging corned beef, Swiss cheese, Russian dressing, and its only redeeming feature, sauerkraut, I shot him a look (right in front of his mother) as if to say **you've got to be kidding me!** As soon as we returned home, I vowed to recreate his childhood favorite with an equally satisfying but healthy duplicate.*

MAKES 2 SANDWICHES

2 tablespoons low-fat Thousand Island dressing

2 tablespoons Orange Puree (see Make-Ahead Recipe #2)

4 slices rye bread

½ pound turkey pastrami or leftover pork tenderloin, sliced

1 cup sauerkraut, well-drained

2 slices low-fat Swiss cheese

Nonstick cooking spray

Alternative to the Thousand Island dressing:

¼ cup Your Honey's Mustard Sauce, page 234

In a large bowl, combine the dressing with Orange Puree (skip this step if using the honey mustard alternative). Spread about a tablespoon of dressing on both sides of each slice of rye bread. Place the turkey or pork slices, sauerkraut, and cheese on two slices of the bread and cover with other slices. If your guy is taking the sandwich to work, wrap it tightly in parchment paper and instruct him to heat it in the microwave for 1 minute before eating.

To grill at home: Generously spray a skillet or griddle with oil and heat to medium. Grill one sandwich at a time, pressing gently on the top of each until the bread is golden brown and the cheese is melted. Flip the sandwich, spraying pan with more oil, and brown the other side for 3 to 4 minutes more. Repeat with the other sandwich.

Sneaky Tip:

Watch out for "panini" grilled sandwiches, the hot new menu item. Most have more fat and calories than an entire personal pizza!

SOUPS

Major Leek Soup

anti oxident boost · *low carb* · *low sugar* · *veggie* · *healthy fats*

If your guy is a Francophile, he's probably familiar with vichyssoise, the delicious artery-clogging soup made of pureed leeks, onions, potatoes, cream, and chicken stock. This Sneaky Chef version has all the taste without the fat, so he can indulge to his heart's content! This soup is traditionally served cold, but feel free to serve it hot if you prefer.

MAKES 4 SERVINGS

1 tablespoon extra-virgin olive oil

3 large leeks, washed and chopped, white and pale green parts only (about 4 cups)

1 small onion, chopped (about 1 cup)

¼ teaspoon salt

2 large russet potatoes (about 1½ pounds), peeled and chopped

3½ to 4 cups low-sodium vegetable or chicken broth

1 cup White Puree (see Make-Ahead Recipe #4)

1 bay leaf

Salt and freshly ground pepper, to taste

Turkey bacon bits, for garnish (optional)

Chopped chives, for garnish (optional)

Heat the oil in a large soup pot over medium heat. Add the leeks, onion, and salt. Cook until tender, about 15 minutes, stirring occasionally to prevent browning. Add the potatoes, broth, White Puree, and bay leaf. Increase heat to high, and bring to a boil. Reduce heat to low, cover, and simmer until the potatoes are tender, about 30 minutes. Discard the bay leaf. Transfer the soup to a blender in batches and puree, or insert a handheld blender directly into the pot.

Stir in salt and a few grinds of pepper. Garnish with a handful of turkey bacon bits and chives, if using. Serve hot or cold.

Beefed-Up Onion Soup

anti oxident boost · low carb · low sugar · omega 3s · healthy fats · veggie

How sneaky can a Sneaky Chef be? In this soup, by caramelizing the onions in pomegranate juice, you can bring out their natural sweetness without using the sugar that's normally found in onion soup. The sweet potato/carrot puree makes the broth extra rich, so no one will miss the extra butter.

For maximum authenticity, serve in an ovenproof crock topped with a whole grain crouton and bubbly low-fat Swiss cheese. Pair with a side salad for a super-satisfying meal.

MAKES 4 SERVINGS

1 tablespoon butter

2 tablespoons extra-virgin olive oil

3 large sweet onions (such as Vidalia), sliced thin (about 6 cups)

$\frac{1}{2}$ teaspoon salt

2 bay leaves

Freshly ground pepper, to taste

1 cup pomegranate juice

3 cups low-sodium beef* broth

1 cup Orange Puree (see Make-Ahead Recipe #2)

Salt, to taste

4 slices whole grain bread, cut into a circle

4 slices low-fat Swiss cheese

Use vegetable broth to make vegetarian

In a large soup pot over moderate heat, melt the butter with oil. Add the onions, salt, bay leaves, and a few grinds of pepper. Cook, stirring often, for about 20 minutes. Add the pomegranate juice and continue cooking onions for another 5 minutes. Add the beef (or vegetable) broth and the Orange Puree and bring to a boil. Reduce the heat to low and simmer, partially covered, for another 20 minutes. Discard the bay leaves. Ladle the soup into 4 soup bowls or ovenproof crocks. Season with salt and additional freshly ground pepper.

To serve authentic French onion soup, gratiné style, place a small round piece of whole grain toast on top of each soup-filled crock. Lay a slice of cheese over top of the entire ovenproof crock and broil on high for 1 to 2 minutes, until cheese is melted and bubbly.

Sneaky Tip:

To avoid scalding your hands when blending hot liquids, let the liquid cool for a few minutes, then fill the blender no more than halfway and cover the closed top with a kitchen towel. Pulse a few times before setting the blender to run on high speed.

Chow Down Chowder

This soup offers a delicious alternative to the creamy chowders that may have been axed from your man's diet during a change to a lower-fat lifestyle. By substituting evaporated skim milk for cream and using White Bean Puree and oat bran as both thickening agents and fiber-boosters, this soup offers a rich, creamy taste and texture with almost no fat.

MAKES 4 SERVINGS

1 tablespoon extra-virgin olive oil

1 medium-size onion, diced (about $\frac{1}{2}$ cup)

$\frac{1}{2}$ teaspoon salt

2 slices turkey bacon, chopped

4 cups vegetable broth

$\frac{1}{2}$ cup White Bean Puree (see Make-Ahead Recipe #9)

$\frac{1}{4}$ cup oat bran

1 russet potato (about $\frac{1}{2}$ pound), diced, with skin

3 cups frozen corn kernels, or the kernels from about 3–4 ears fresh corn, cut off cob

1 cup evaporated skim milk

Freshly ground pepper, to taste

Optional extra boost: 2 celery ribs, diced; and/or 1 red bell pepper, diced

Heat the oil in a large soup pot over medium heat. Cook the onions until they are slightly translucent, about 10 minutes, and then add the celery and bell pepper (if using), sautéing for another 5 minutes. Add the turkey bacon, cooking about 5 minutes more. Add the vegetable broth, White Bean Puree, oat bran, and potato. Increase the heat and bring to a boil, then immediately reduce the heat to low, cover, and simmer for about 30 minutes or until the potatoes are tender. Add the corn and the evaporated milk and cook for another 5 minutes. Ladle into 4 soup bowls and season with freshly ground pepper to taste.

Sneaky Tip:

The Archives of Internal Medicine predicts that the average diabetic American man will live to be 72 years old, versus 79 for healthy males.

Sneaky Tip:

Penn State researchers found that eating a low-calorie soup before a meal can reduce your overall calorie intake by 20 percent, helping you manage weight.

Cheddar Jalapeño Variation

Follow the instructions for Chow Down Chowder, but top each bowl of soup with 2 tablespoons of low-fat shredded cheddar cheese and a handful of chopped jalapeño peppers.

Crabmeat Variation

Follow the instructions for Chow Down Chowder, but top each bowl of soup with 2 tablespoons of cooked lump crabmeat.

Manhattan Clam Chowder

(anti oxident boost) (low sugar) (omega 3s) (healthy fats) (protein boost)

I served this dish at a clambake last summer, and my doctor friend, Tassos (a true foodie), proclaimed it the best clam chowder he'd ever tasted. When I revealed the secret healthy ingredients and the fact that it's nearly fat free, he was so impressed that he took out his prescription pad and prescribed this soup as a new heart medicine!

The hidden sardines not only boost the omega-3s, but subtly enhance the clam flavor.

MAKES 4 SERVINGS

1 tablespoon extra-virgin olive oil

1 medium-size onion, diced (about 1 cup)

½ teaspoon salt

3 to 4 garlic cloves, minced

½ cup White or Orange Puree
   (see Make-Ahead Recipe #4 or #2)

1 (6-ounce) can tomato paste

3 (8-ounce) bottles clam juice

1 (28-ounce) can diced, peeled tomatoes,
   with liquid

1 large russet potato,* diced, with skin

2 (6½-ounce) cans chopped clams, with liquid

1 (3- to 4-ounce) can skinless and boneless
   sardines, packed in water, drained

Freshly ground black pepper, to taste

Dried red pepper flakes, to taste

Optional extra boost: **2 celery ribs, diced**

Sneaky Time Saving Tip:

Use low-fat frozen hash browns instead of dicing fresh potatoes

Heat the oil in a large soup pot over medium heat. Add the onion and salt and sauté until they are slightly translucent, about 10 minutes. Add the celery (if using) and sauté for another 5 minutes. Add the garlic, White or Orange Puree, tomato paste, clam juice, diced tomatoes, potato, and clams with their liquid. Stir to combine well. Add the sardines, breaking them up with the spoon, slightly mashing them into the pot so there are no remaining visible pieces. Bring to a boil, then reduce heat to medium-low, cover, and simmer for about 30 minutes or until the potatoes are tender. Ladle into 4 soup bowls, and season with freshly ground pepper and red pepper flakes.

Appetizers and Side Dishes

Boosted Buffalo Wings

anti oxident boost · indulge · low carb · low sugar · protein boost

Eating wings is one of the ultimate guy rituals. Men love to one-up each other on how fiery they can stand them and how messy they can get. Let the men in your life occasionally enjoy this sneaky treat, while we enjoy watching them unknowingly lick cauliflower and zucchini puree off their sticky fingers! These wings go great with the not-so-classic Bountiful Blue Cheese Dressing (page 239), which is loaded with White Puree and low-fat ricotta.

MAKES 4 SERVINGS

½ cup White Puree (see Make-Ahead Recipe #4)

1 cup store-bought barbecue sauce or 1½ cups Homemade BBQ Sauce*, page 226

Hot sauce to taste

4 pounds buffalo chicken wings (about 32 pieces)

Salt and freshly ground pepper, to taste

Celery Ribs, cut into sticks

1 cup Bountiful Blue Cheese Dressing, page 239

If you are using Homemade BBQ Sauce, omit the White Puree called for in this recipe.

Preheat the oven to 425 degrees. Spray a baking sheet with oil.

In a large bowl, mix the White Puree with the barbecue sauce (omit this step if using Homemade BBQ Sauce). Add the hot sauce to taste and set sauce aside.

Spread wings on prepared baking sheet and season with salt and pepper. Cook for 30 minutes, then remove from oven and brush on the sauce. Continue cooking for another 5 to 10 minutes, until nicely browned.

Serve with celery sticks and Bountiful Blue Cheese Dressing.

Concealed Crab Cakes

I can't think of a tastier way to give your man a good dose of fiber and omega-3s than with these authentic yet low-fat crab cakes. Put on a Jimmy Buffet disc and your favorite sundress and you'll feel like you're in Key West for a romantic getaway.

MAKES 8 CRAB CAKES

1 tablespoon light mayonnaise

1 egg white

¼ cup White Bean Puree (see Make-Ahead Recipe #9)

1 tablespoon Dijon or coarse-grain mustard

¼ to ½ teaspoon hot sauce

1 teaspoon Old Bay Seasoning

⅓ plus ⅓ cup wheat germ

Freshly ground pepper

½ pound fresh lump crabmeat (about 2 cups), drained

Optional extra boost: handful of chopped green onions, celery, and/or bell peppers

Preheat the oven to 400 degrees. Spray a baking sheet with oil.

In a medium-size bowl, whisk the egg white, then mix in the White Bean Puree, mustard, hot sauce, Old Bay, ⅓ cup of the wheat germ, a few grinds of pepper, and the crabmeat.

Pour the remaining ⅓ cup of wheat germ on a plate. Scoop about ⅓ cup of crab mixture and form it into a fairly thick cake. Dredge the cakes in the wheat germ, fully covering all sides of the cake, and place the crab cake on the prepared baking sheet. Repeat with remaining crab mixture. Spray the top side of the cakes with oil and bake for 10 minutes. Flip once, spray oil on the tops of the cakes, and bake for another 8 to 10 minutes, until golden brown.

Serve cakes with a lemon wedges and Side of Slaw, page 185.

Sneaky Tip:

In a study of happily married couples, psychologists from the University of Virginia found that holding hands with your spouse may help you reduce stress.

10 SIMPLE TIPS FOR MAKING YOUR KITCHEN MORE ENERGY EFFICIENT

1. Replace regular light bulbs with energy-efficient compact fluorescent bulbs.
2. Move your thermostat up 2 degrees in summer and down 2 degrees in winter.
3. Run your dishwasher only with a full load.
4. Keep your water heater thermostat no higher than 120°F.
5. Buy products with less packaging, and recycle paper, plastic, and glass.
6. Replace old appliances—inefficient appliances waste energy.
7. Unplug small appliances when you leave the room.
8. Turn off fans and lights when you leave the room.
9. Bring cloth bags to the market to reduce your use of plastic and paper (or at least reuse the paper and plastic bags you get there).
10. Buy locally grown and organic food whenever possible.

Quick Fixes for Canned Baked Beans

Each of the boosters below enhances the nutritional profile of canned baked beans. You can mix in one or both of these boosters at once, but keep the ratio at no more than ½ cup per 16-ounce can of beans to remain above suspicion.

**EACH OF THE FOLLOWING QUICK FIXES IS FOR
1 (16-OUNCE) CAN OF BAKED BEANS**

* ¼ to ½ cup White Puree (see Make-Ahead Recipe #4)

Prepare the baked beans according to the directions on the can. Add the White Puree to the beans, mixing until well blended.

* ¼ to ½ cup Orange Puree (see Make-Ahead Recipe #2)

Prepare the baked beans according to the directions on the can. Add the Orange Puree to the beans, mixing until well blended.

Sneaky Tip:

Exposure to secondhand smoke can double the number of wrinkles on your body.

Rosemary-Olive Biscotti

anti oxident boost · low sugar · omega 3s · veggie · whole grains · healthy fats · protein boost

These crispy, savory cookies boast hidden pureed chickpeas, a little olive oil, and a dose of whole grains. They're great by themselves with a glass of wine, dipped into soup, or broken up as croutons on your salad. Make a few batches at a time and keep leftovers on hand in a freezer bag. I've even caught my husband munching on them frozen, but for the best flavor, you'll want to let them defrost first!

MAKES ABOUT 12 BISCOTTI

1 large egg

⅓ cup White Bean Puree or Chickpea Puree
   (see Make-Ahead Recipe #9 or #10)

2 tablespoons grated Parmesan cheese

½ cup shredded low-fat cheddar cheese

1 garlic clove, minced

¾ cup Flour Blend (see Make-Ahead
   Recipe #13)

½ teaspoon salt

¼ teaspoon onion powder

1 teaspoon baking powder

Salt and freshly ground pepper, to taste

1 tablespoon chopped fresh rosemary,
   or 1 teaspoon dried

¼ cup roughly chopped kalamata olives

Preheat the oven to 375 degrees. Line a baking sheet with parchment paper (or spray with oil).

In a large bowl, combine the egg, White Bean or Chickpea Puree, Parmesan cheese, cheddar cheese, and garlic. In another bowl, whisk together the Flour Blend, salt, onion powder, baking powder, and a few grinds of pepper. Add the dry ingredients to the wet and mix just enough to moisten the dry ingredients. Stir in the rosemary and olives.

Place the dough on the prepared baking sheet and use your fingers to form a log approximately 4 inches wide x 9 inches long. Bake for 20 minutes, remove from the oven, and let cool for 5 minutes.

Place the log on a cutting board. Using a serrated knife, cut the log into ½-inch thick diagonal slices. Place the slices back on the baking sheet, spray the biscotti with oil, sprinkle with salt, and bake for another 15 minutes. Flip the biscotti over, spray with oil, sprinkle with salt, and bake for a final 15 minutes, until nicely browned.

Serve with a glass of wine or a hot bowl of soup, for dipping.

Better Batter Onion Rings

(anti oxident boost) (low carb) (low sugar) (veggie) (whole grains) (healthy fats)

Guys go to a steakhouse and think they're doing themselves a favor by ordering an onion blossom as an appetizer. The only problem is that this "vegetable" consists of one large, batter-dipped, deep-fried onion weighing in at an astounding 2000+ calories and more than 100 grams of fat! For a satisfying substitute, try these low-fat, high-fiber, oven-fried onion rings, with a crispy coating of cornmeal and ground almonds.

MAKES ABOUT 4 SERVINGS

$\frac{1}{4}$ cup whole grain flour

$\frac{1}{4}$ teaspoon salt

2 egg whites

$\frac{1}{2}$ cup White Puree (see Make-Ahead Recipe #4)

$\frac{1}{4}$ cup Ground Almonds (see Make-Ahead Recipe #14)

$\frac{1}{2}$ cup cornmeal

$\frac{1}{2}$ teaspoon paprika

Pinch to $\frac{1}{4}$ teaspoon cayenne (optional)

Salt and freshly ground pepper, to taste

1 large onion, cut into $\frac{1}{2}$-inch rings

Preheat the oven to 425 degrees. Spray a baking sheet with oil.

Combine the flour and salt in a shallow dish or plate. In another shallow dish, beat together the egg whites and the White Puree and set the mixture next to the flour. In a third shallow bowl or plate, combine the ground almonds, cornmeal, paprika, cayenne, salt and freshly ground pepper; mix well.

Separate the onion slices into rings. Dredge each onion ring in the flour, shake off the excess, then dip in the egg mixture, and then in the cornmeal mixture. Press the breading evenly onto both sides of the rings.

Place the breaded onion rings on the prepared baking sheet. Spray the top side of the onions with oil and bake for about 20 minutes. With a spatula, turn the rings over once, spray the tops with oil, and then return to the oven for another 15 to 20 minutes, until the coating is lightly browned and crisp.

Sneaky Tip:

A German study tracked 184,000 people for eight years and found that those whose diets contained significant amounts of onions, apples and berries high in the compounds quercetin and flavonoids were 23 percent less likely to develop pancreatic cancer. These compounds destroy cancer cells, preventing them from spreading throughout the body.

Don't-Be-Sorry Calamari

anti oxident boost · low carb · low sugar · omega 3s · whole grains · healthy fats · protein boost

The ultimate bar food and a staple in Greek and Italian cuisine, fried calamari is often served as an appetizer alongside a spicy, fat-filled dip. I managed to keep this finger food's crunch appeal intact by coating the calamari with a nutritious mixture of cornmeal and ground almonds, then baking them at a high temperature with just a mist of olive oil to provide a deep-fried taste and texture. You can sneak four more veggies into this snack if you serve the Mega Marinara Sauce, page 228, on the side as a dip.

MAKES 4 APPETIZER SERVINGS

$\frac{1}{4}$ cup whole grain flour

$\frac{1}{4}$ teaspoon salt

2 egg whites

$\frac{1}{2}$ cup White Puree (see Make-Ahead Recipe #4)

$\frac{1}{4}$ cup Ground Almonds (see Make-Ahead Recipe #14)

$\frac{1}{2}$ cup cornmeal

$\frac{1}{2}$ teaspoon paprika

Pinch to $\frac{1}{4}$ teaspoon cayenne (optional)

Freshly ground pepper, to taste

1 pound cleaned calamari (squid), with tentacles intact, bodies cut into $\frac{1}{2}$-inch-thick rings

2 lemons, cut into wedges

Preheat the oven to 425 degrees. Spray a baking sheet with oil.

Combine the flour and salt in a shallow dish or plate. In another shallow dish, beat together the egg whites and the White Puree and set the mixture next to the flour. In a third shallow dish or plate, combine the ground almonds, cornmeal, paprika, cayenne, and freshly ground pepper; mix well.

Dredge a small batch of calamari pieces in the flour and shake off the excess. Dip the calamari in the egg mixture, and then in the cornmeal mixture. Press the breading evenly onto all sides of the calamari.

Place the breaded calamari on the prepared baking sheet. Spray the top of the calamari with oil and bake for about 20 minutes. With a spatula, turn the pieces over once, spray with oil, and then return the baking sheet to the oven for another 15 to 20 minutes, until the coating is lightly browned and crisp.

Serve with lemon wedges and a small bowl of Mega Marinara Sauce, page 228, as a dip.

Mighty Mashed Potatoes, 5 Sneaky Ways

These mashed potatoes are more than comfort food reserved for major holidays. With these revamped recipes, we can enjoy them whenever the mood strikes. Here are five low-fat variations, a different decoy flavor for every night of the week, that all feature hidden cauliflower, zucchini, and plain yogurt, with just a touch of heart healthy olive oil. You can slowly increase the ratio of White Puree to potato if your man doesn't object to a more noticeable vegetable taste.

While you can use either Yukon gold or russet potatoes for these recipes, remember that russets took top honors among foods high in antioxidants.

If there are any leftovers, use them atop the Potato-Crusted Meatloaf Variation of Not His Mother's Meatloaf, page 263.

Parmesan Mashed Potatoes

MAKES 4 TO 6 SERVINGS

2 pounds Yukon gold or russet potatoes (about 4 medium-sized potatoes), peeled and quartered

3 tablespoons grated Parmesan cheese

½ cup White Puree or White Bean Puree (see Make-Ahead Recipe #4 or #9)

½ cup low-fat plain yogurt

2 tablespoons extra-virgin olive oil

½ teaspoon salt

Freshly ground pepper, to taste

Optional extra boost: Chopped chives

Place the potatoes in a large pot of cold, salted water and bring to a boil. Lower the heat, cover, and simmer for 25 to 35 minutes, until the potatoes are completely tender. Drain the potatoes into a colander, then return them to the pot. Add the Parmesan, the White Puree or White Bean Puree, and the yogurt,

olive oil, salt, and pepper. Mash with a potato masher until well combined. Add a bit more yogurt if needed. Garnish with the chives, if using. Serve immediately, or keep the mashed potatoes hot on the stovetop in a metal bowl set over simmering water.

Roasted Garlic Mashed Potatoes

MAKES 4 TO 6 SERVINGS

2 pounds Yukon gold or russet potatoes (about 4 medium-sized potatoes), peeled and quartered

2 to 3 heads garlic

$\frac{1}{2}$ cup White Puree or White Bean Puree (see Make-Ahead Recipe #4 or #9)

$\frac{1}{2}$ cup low-fat plain yogurt

2 tablespoons extra-virgin olive oil

$\frac{1}{2}$ teaspoon salt

Freshly ground pepper, to taste

Optional extra boost: 3 tablespoons chopped chives

Preheat the oven to 350 degrees.

Place the potatoes in a large pot of cold, salted water and bring to a boil. Lower the heat, cover, and simmer for 25 to 35 minutes, until the potatoes are completely tender.

Meanwhile, wrap the garlic heads in foil and roast them in the oven for 30 minutes. Remove the garlic from the oven and squeeze the garlic flesh out of the skins.

Drain the potatoes into a colander, then return them to the pot. Add the roasted garlic flesh, the White Puree or White Bean Puree, and the yogurt, olive oil, salt, and pepper.

Mash with a potato masher until well combined. Add a bit more yogurt if needed. Garnish with the chives, if using. Serve immediately, or keep the mashed potatoes hot on the stovetop in a metal bowl set over simmering water.

Bacon-and-Cheddar Mashed Potatoes

MAKES 4 TO 6 SERVINGS

2 pounds Yukon gold or russet potatoes (about 4 medium-sized potatoes), peeled and quartered

½ cup low-fat buttermilk

½ cup shredded low-fat cheddar cheese

3 tablespoons Bacon Bits (see Make-Ahead Recipe #16)

½ cup White Puree or White Bean Puree (see Make-Ahead Recipe #4 or #10)

2 tablespoons extra-virgin olive oil

½ teaspoon salt

Freshly ground pepper, to taste

Optional extra boost: **chopped chives**

Place the potatoes in a large pot of cold, salted water and bring to a boil. Lower the heat, cover, and simmer for 25 to 35 minutes, until the potatoes are completely tender. Drain the potatoes into a colander, then return them to the pot. Add the buttermilk, cheese, bacon bits, White Puree or White Bean Puree, olive oil, salt, and pepper. Mash with a potato masher until well combined. Add a bit more buttermilk if needed. Garnish with the chives, if using. Serve immediately, or keep the mashed potatoes hot on the stovetop in a metal bowl set over simmering water.

Chipotle Mashed Potatoes

anti oxident boost   low sugar   veggie   healthy fats

Because of the red color of this dish, I recommend using small red skin potatoes, leaving their skins on for added flavor and nutrition. I've also added an extra quarter cup of White Puree to this variation, since the chipotles are so good at hiding its flavor.

MAKES 4 TO 6 SERVINGS

2 pounds red skin potatoes (about 4 medium-sized potatoes), quartered, with skins left on

$3/4$ cup White Puree or White Bean Puree (see Make-Ahead Recipe #4 or #9)

$1/2$ cup low-fat plain yogurt

2 tablespoons extra-virgin olive oil

1 to 2 tablespoons chipotle peppers in adobo sauce*

$1/2$ teaspoon salt

Freshly ground pepper, to taste

Canned chipotle peppers in adobo sauce are sold in the Mexican section of most grocery stores.

Place the potatoes in a large pot of cold, salted water and bring to a boil. Lower the heat, cover, and simmer for 25 to 35 minutes, until the potatoes are completely tender. Drain the potatoes into a colander, then return them to the pot. Add the White Puree or White Bean Puree, yogurt, olive oil, chipotles with sauce, salt, and pepper. Mash with a potato masher until well combined. Add a bit more yogurt if needed. Serve immediately, or keep the mashed potatoes hot on the stovetop in a metal bowl set over simmering water.

Pesto Mashed Potatoes

In this variation, the pesto eliminates the need for additional olive oil, salt, or yogurt.

MAKES 4 TO 6 SERVINGS

2 pounds Yukon gold or russet potatoes (about 4 medium-sized potatoes), peeled and quartered

½ cup store-bought pesto*, or 1 cup Perfect Pesto, page 223

½ cup Green Puree (see Make-Ahead Recipe #3)

Freshly ground pepper, to taste

Optional extra boost: **Chopped chives**

If you are using Perfect Pesto, omit the Green Puree called for in this recipe.

Place the potatoes in a large pot of cold, salted water and bring to a boil. Lower the heat, cover, and simmer for 25 to 35 minutes, until the potatoes are completely tender. Drain the potatoes into a colander, then return them to the pot. Add the pesto and Green Puree, if necessary. Mash with a potato masher until well combined. Garnish with the chives, if using. Serve immediately, or keep the mashed potatoes hot on the stovetop in a metal bowl set over simmering water.

Real Freedom Fries

My husband and kids like to claim they've had their "vegetables" after they've eaten French fries with ketchup, and the truth is, they're sort of correct. We still need our greens and other veggies, but let's not overlook the nutritional value of America's favorite fried potato. The lowly russet potato surprised the health community and took top honors for its disease-fighting, antioxidant rating—and underneath all the processing, ketchup still comes from tomatoes, though singing ketchup's praises is a bit more of a stretch.

As in the kids' book, I've made these low-fat fries with a touch of heart-healthy olive oil and a dusting of cornmeal, which mimics the texture of the deep-fried variety. The cornmeal also adds a little extra fiber and whole grain nutrition. Egg whites cut down on the need for a lot of oil, and they also help the potatoes achieve a nice golden crust. Feel free to adjust the amount of spice in this recipe to suit your taste.

To create a French bistro feeling, serve these fries in an ice cream parfait glass lined with parchment paper sticking out of the top.

MAKES 4 SERVINGS

4 russet potatoes (about 2 pounds)

2 egg whites

2 tablespoons extra-virgin olive oil

½ teaspoon salt

2 tablespoons cornmeal

Optional spice mixture: ¼ teaspoon chili powder; ¼ teaspoon cumin; and/or ¼ teaspoon cayenne

Preheat the oven to 400 degrees. Spray a baking sheet with oil.

Cut each potato into 8 wedges or several thin sticks. In a large bowl, toss the potatoes with the egg whites, olive oil, and salt, coating evenly. Dust the potatoes with the cornmeal and the spice mixture, if using, and spread them in a single layer on the baking sheet.

Bake 50 to 60 minutes or until golden brown. Serve American style, with ketchup, or British style, sprinkled with malt vinegar.

Goes well with Something's Fishy Sticks, page 273, Now You're Talkin' Turkey Burgers, page 279, or Barbell Burgers, page 287.

Chili Fry Variation

Follow the instructions for Real Freedom Fries, but serve the fries covered in Doctor's Choice Chili, page 261, and a sprinkling of shredded low-fat cheddar cheese.

Sneaky Tip:

A recent four-year study conducted by Johns Hopkins University revealed that more than two-thirds of Americans are starving themselves of necessary nutrients. Even when trans fat—laden French fries were counted as a vegetable, the majority of Americans eat fewer than one-third the recommended servings of fruits and veggies each day.

Baked Clams

anti oxident boost · low carb · low sugar · omega 3s · whole grains · healthy fats · protein boost

*Mmm. Baked Clams **Oreganate** are favorite hors d'oeuvre at cocktail parties. Now your man can indulge in them on the first day of a healthy eating program, because I've replaced the white bread-crumbs and butter with a satisfying topping of whole grain cornmeal and ground almonds, held together with a bit of cauliflower/zucchini puree and a dash of heart-healthy olive oil.*

MAKES 1 DOZEN CLAMS

1 dozen fresh littleneck or small cherrystone clams

2 tablespoons cornmeal, plus additional for flushing out clams

Salt, for flushing out clams

2 tablespoons Ground Almonds (see Make-Ahead Recipe #14)

1 tablespoon Parmesan cheese

1 to 2 garlic cloves, minced

$\frac{1}{2}$ teaspoon chopped fresh or dried oregano

$1\frac{1}{2}$ tablespoons extra-virgin olive oil

1 tablespoon lemon juice

Freshly ground pepper, to taste

Optional garnish: 2 tablespoons crumbled turkey bacon bits

Note: I choose to lightly steam the clams so their shells open easily, rather than risk prying open hard shells on raw clams. However, if you are comfortable shucking clams, omit the boiling step, shuck the raw clams, and proceed with the recipe, adding 3 to 5 minutes to the broiling time.

Rinse the clams very well in a colander, or place them in a bucket of cold water with a handful of cornmeal and salt to flush out the sand.

In a large pot, bring 1 cup of water to a boil, add the clams, cover, and cook for 5 minutes. Remove all open clams with tongs or a slotted spoon and continue to boil those that haven't opened. After a total of 8 minutes, discard any remaining unopened clams.

Preheat the broiler. While waiting for the clams to cool enough to handle, in a medium-size bowl mix together the 2 tablespoons cornmeal, the ground almonds, Parmesan, garlic, oregano, olive oil, lemon juice, and a few grinds of pepper.

Fully open the clams, separating the shells, and place the half of the shell with the clam inside it on a baking sheet. Discard the other clam shells. Put about 1 heaping teaspoon of the cornmeal mixture on each clam. Garnish with the bacon bits, if using. Spray the tops of the clams with oil and broil for 2 to 3 minutes, until golden brown. Serve immediately.

Sneaky Tip:

Add some fresh oregano to your red sauce. Government research has found that chopped fresh oregano stops oxidative damage that can lead to cancer. Ounce for ounce, oregano even outshines the health benefits of blueberries.

Steakhouse Salad with Blue Cheese and Bacon

anti oxident boost · low carb · low sugar · healthy fats · protein boost

Blue cheese and bacon dressing make this a classic steakhouse favorite. The crunch and size of the iceberg wedge makes it very popular with guys and easy for us to prepare—one slice with a knife and you're done! Although iceberg isn't nearly as nutritionally dense as romaine, here it serves a purpose; its mild flavor, satisfying crunch, and bulk make it look like a lot of food. It also takes time to eat and slows down the meal.

MAKES 2 SERVINGS

1 head iceberg lettuce, cut into 2 wedges

¼ cup Bountiful Blue Cheese Dressing, page 239

2 tablespoons crumbled turkey bacon

Freshly ground pepper

Optional extra boost:

a few thin slices of red onion

Arrange each wedge of lettuce on a plate and drizzle 2 tablespoons of blue cheese dressing onto each. Garnish each wedge with 1 tablespoon of crumbled bacon, a few grinds of black pepper, and the red onion, if using.

Sneaky Tip:

Here's a great motivator. According to a Harvard University study, men who exercise 3 to 5 hours a week have a 30 percent lower risk of developing erectile dysfunction (impotence).

Don't Fret Fritters

anti oxident boost · whole grains · veggie · healthy fats

You don't have to wait for National Corn Fritter Day (July 16th!) to enjoy these Southern treats. Traditionally battered and deep-fried, this sneaky recipe adds four hidden veggies and two whole grains to the favorite dish, all while managing to keep the classic look and taste intact.

MAKES 18 TO 20 FRITTERS

2 egg whites

$\frac{1}{2}$ cup White Puree (see Make-Ahead Recipe #4)

$\frac{1}{2}$ small onion, finely chopped (about $\frac{1}{2}$ cup)

1 cup corn kernels, fresh or frozen

$\frac{1}{4}$ cup low-fat sweetened condensed milk

$\frac{1}{2}$ teaspoon salt

$\frac{1}{2}$ cup cornmeal

$\frac{1}{2}$ cup whole wheat flour, plus additional as needed

$\frac{1}{4}$ to $\frac{1}{2}$ cup chopped jalapeño peppers (about 1–2 jalapeños)

Freshly ground pepper, to taste

5 teaspoons extra-virgin olive oil

Whisk the egg whites in a medium-size bowl. Mix in the White Puree, onion, corn, condensed milk, and salt. Mix in the cornmeal, flour, jalapeño peppers, and freshly ground pepper.

Coat a large skillet with cooking spray. Heat the skillet over medium-high heat, then add 1 teaspoon of the olive oil. Turn the heat down to medium if the oil starts to smoke.

Drop four single tablespoonfuls of batter onto the hot skillet, gently flattening each with a spatula. Cook until browned on one side, about 4 minutes. Turn the fritters over with a spatula and cook the other sides until golden brown, another 2 to 3 minutes. Repeat with the next batch of 4 fritters, adding more oil to the pan as needed. Place the cooked fritters on a plate lined with paper towels to blot away excess oil.

Sauces and Salad Dressings

Perfect Pesto

Pesto is a pretty healthy sauce to begin with, but a few sneaky substitutions bump it into the all-star category. Vegetable broth knocks out half the fat of traditional pesto, and the extra green veggies will slip right under your man's veggie-detecting radar screen.

This is a great lunch pail choice, since it can be served cold. Toss some whole grain pasta in the sauce, and place it in a plastic container for your guy's lunch.

Some other serving suggestions: Toss with any shaped pasta or spaghetti, add a dollop to soups, spread on whole grain bread topped with sliced tomato, or use as a cold sauce for simple grilled chicken, fish, or steak.

MAKES ABOUT 2 CUPS OF PESTO

6 cups fresh basil leaves, rinsed and packed

½ cup walnuts

4 to 6 garlic cloves, chopped

½ teaspoon salt

2 teaspoons lemon juice

½ cup vegetable broth

½ cup Green Puree (see Make-Ahead Recipe #3)

Freshly ground pepper, to taste

½ cup walnut oil or extra-virgin olive oil

½ cup Parmesan or Romano cheese

Place the basil in the bowl of your food processor and pulse a few times. Add the walnuts, garlic, salt, lemon juice, vegetable broth, Green Puree, and a few grinds of pepper. Puree on high until smooth. With the processor running, slowly stream the oil through the processor's feed tube. Add the cheese and puree for another few seconds. Use or store immediately. The pesto will keep in the refrigerator for 3 days, or in the freezer for 3 months. Before storing, cover the top of the container with a thin layer of olive oil to keep the pesto from oxidizing and turning brown.

Date Night Variation

Follow the instructions for Perfect Pesto, but omit the garlic.

Sneaky Tip:

Don't drive him to the train station! Researchers at Indiana University concur with studies indicating that several brief bouts of exercise each day offer health benefits that are similar to a continuous workout that lasts the same total amount of time.

Quick Fixes for Store-Bought Salsa

Each of the boosters below enhances the nutritional profile of store-bought salsa. You can mix in one or both of the boosters below, up to a total of about one-quarter cup booster per cup of salsa.

EACH OF THE FOLLOWING QUICK FIXES IS FOR ½ CUP OF SALSA

* 2 to 4 tablespoons White Puree
   (see Make-Ahead Recipe #4)

Add the White Puree to the salsa, mixing until well blended.

* 2 to 4 tablespoons Orange Puree
   (see Make-Ahead Recipe #2)

Add the Orange Puree to the salsa, mixing until well blended.

Homemade BBQ Sauce

Barbecue sauce is such a manly staple that it begs to be used as a carrier for some healthy ingredients! This quick and versatile sauce can be made as spicy as desired.

MAKES ALMOST 2 CUPS OF SAUCE

1 green tea bag

$\frac{3}{4}$ cup tomato paste

$\frac{1}{2}$ cup cider vinegar

$\frac{3}{4}$ cup White or Orange Puree (see Make-Ahead Recipe #4 or #2)

1 to 2 garlic cloves, minced

Freshly ground pepper, to taste

$\frac{1}{2}$ teaspoon salt

2 tablespoons Worcestershire sauce

2 tablespoons honey

2 to 3 teaspoons chili powder

Hot sauce, to taste

Steep the tea bags in $\frac{1}{2}$ cup boiling water for 2 minutes (no longer or it will taste bitter). Allow the tea to cool, then whisk a $\frac{1}{2}$ cup of tea together with the tomato paste, vinegar, White or Orange Puree, garlic, pepper, salt, Worcestershire sauce, and honey. Add the chili powder and hot sauce to taste. Thin with more green tea if desired.

Cover and store in the refrigerator for up to 3 days.

Quick Fixes for Store-Bought Barbecue Sauce

Each of the boosters below both enhances the nutritional profile of your man's favorite bottled barbecue sauce. In addition, they cut the sauce's acidity, which may help to prevent acid reflux. Start by adding the smallest recommended amount of just one of the nutritional boosters, and add a little more each time you serve the sauce. You can also mix in two or more of the boosters below, up to a total of about ½ cup booster per 1 cup of store-bought barbecue sauce.

EACH OF THE FOLLOWING QUICK FIXES IS FOR ½ CUP OF BOTTLED BARBECUE SAUCE

* 2 to 4 tablespoons Green Juice
   (see Make-Ahead Recipe #5)
Combine the Green Juice with store-bought barbecue sauce, mixing until well blended. The juice makes the sauce a little thinner, so this variation is best for basting and in marinades.

* 2 to 4 tablespoons White Bean Puree
   (see Make-Ahead Recipe #9)
Combine the White Bean Puree with the store-bought sauce, mixing until well blended.

* 2 to 4 tablespoons White Puree
   (see Make-Ahead Recipe #4)

Combine the White Puree with the store-bought sauce, mixing until well blended.

* 2 to 4 tablespoons Orange Puree
   (see Make-Ahead Recipe #2)
Combine the Orange Puree with the store-bought sauce, mixing until well blended.

* 2 to 4 tablespoons Blueberry Juice
   (see Make-Ahead Recipe #6)
Combine the Blueberry Juice with the store-bought sauce, mixing until well blended. The juice makes the sauce a little thinner, so this variation is best for basting and in marinades.

Mega Marinara Sauce

anti oxident boost · low carb · low sugar · veggie · healthy fats

I used to think making a good homemade marinara was a secret known only to little old Italian grandmas who started with tomatoes from their garden and spent the whole day peeling and simmering them into a hearty sauce. Thanks to incredible canned Italian plum tomatoes, especially the San Marzanos variety, you can accomplish a similar taste in just under a half hour. This versatile sauce makes the world's best hiding place for your sneaky purees, and it can be used in any recipe that calls for marinara or tomato sauce.

MAKES ABOUT 4 CUPS SAUCE

2 tablespoons extra-virgin olive oil

1 medium-size onion, finely minced or pureed (about 1½ cups)

2 to 3 garlic cloves, finely minced

1 (28-ounce) can whole peeled tomatoes with liquid

1 (6-ounce) can tomato paste

2 teaspoons dried basil

1 teaspoon dried oregano

⅛ teaspoon dried red pepper flakes

⅓ cup Orange Puree (see Make-Ahead Recipe #2)

⅓ cup White Puree (see Make-Ahead Recipe #4)

½ teaspoon salt

Freshly ground pepper, to taste

Heat the oil in a deep saucepan over medium heat. Add the onions and garlic and cook, stirring occasionally, until the onions are slightly translucent but not brown. Mix in the tomatoes, tomato paste, basil, oregano, red pepper flakes, Orange Puree, and White Puree, and bring to a boil. Lower the heat and simmer 15 to 20 minutes, until the sauce thickens. Transfer the sauce to a blender in batches, filling it no more than halfway at a time. Puree, pulsing a few times before turning the blender on high, or insert a handheld blender directly into the pot. Stir in the salt and several grinds of pepper. Use immediately, or cover and store in the refrigerator for up to 1 week, or freeze for up to 6 months.

Vodka Sauce Variation

Follow the instructions for Mega Marinara Sauce, but at the very end, add one 5-ounce can (about $\frac{3}{4}$ cup) of evaporated low-fat milk and $\frac{1}{4}$ cup of vodka to the saucepan mixing until well blended. Simmer about 5 minutes to thicken the sauce and burn off the alcohol, then puree the sauce as instructed above. Vodka sauce is traditionally served with penne pasta.

Quick Fixes for Store-Bought Tomato Sauce

Each of the boosters below enhances the nutritional profile of your family's favorite bottled pasta sauce. In addition, they cut the acidity of the tomatoes, which may help to prevent acid reflux. Each booster has proven to be undetectable in taste, and any slight change in color can quickly be reversed by adding a little canned tomato paste. Start by adding the smallest recommended amount of just one of the nutritional boosters, and add a little more each time you serve the sauce. You can also mix in two or more of the boosters below, up to a total of about ½ cup booster per 1 cup of store-bought tomato sauce.

EACH OF THE FOLLOWING QUICK FIXES IS FOR 1 CUP OF BOTTLED SAUCE

* 2 to 4 tablespoons White Bean Puree (see Make-Ahead Recipe #9)

Combine the White Bean Puree with the store-bought sauce, mixing until well blended. If the sauce becomes too light, mix in some canned tomato paste, a tablespoon at a time, to bring the color back to a deeper red.

* 2 to 4 tablespoons White Puree (see Make-Ahead Recipe #4)

Combine the White Puree with the store-bought sauce, mixing until well blended. If the sauce becomes too light, mix in some canned tomato paste, a tablespoon at a time, to bring the color back to a deeper red.

* 2 to 4 tablespoons Orange Puree (see Make-Ahead Recipe #2)

Combine the Orange Puree with the store-bought sauce, mixing until well blended. If the sauce becomes too light, mix in some canned tomato paste, a tablespoon at a time, to bring the color back to a deeper red.

* ¼ cup evaporated skim milk

Combine the evaporated milk with the store-bought sauce, mixing until well blended. This sauce will be closer to pink in color.

Basic Marinade for Chicken, Fish, or Pork

MAKES 1 CUP MARINADE, ENOUGH FOR ABOUT 2 POUNDS OF MEAT

2 garlic cloves, minced

2 tablespoons low-sodium
soy sauce

½ cup pomegranate or
cranberry juice

2 tablespoons freshly
squeezed lemon juice

2 tablespoons extra-virgin
olive oil

2 teaspoons Dijon mustard

1 teaspoon onion powder

Freshly ground pepper,
to taste

In a medium-size bowl, whisk together all the ingredients. Cover and store in the refrigerator for up to 3 days.

Basic Marinade for Beef

MAKES 1 CUP MARINADE, ENOUGH FOR ABOUT 2 POUNDS OF MEAT

2 tablespoons Worcestershire sauce

2 tablespoons balsamic vinegar

2 garlic cloves, minced

1 teaspoon onion powder

2 tablespoons low-sodium soy sauce

2 tablespoons extra-virgin olive oil

$\frac{1}{2}$ cup pomegranate or cranberry juice

Freshly ground pepper, to taste

In a medium-size bowl, whisk together all the ingredients. Cover and store in the refrigerator for up to 3 days.

My favorite animal is steak.

—*Fran Lebowitz*

HEALTH TIPS FOR MEAT

A Cornell University study found that women eat sweets to ward off the blues, but men turn to meat when they want to indulge.

According to the latest government data, a three-ounce serving of the six leanest beef cuts averages just one more gram of saturated fat than a serving of skinless chicken breast.

Beef contains conjugated linoleic acid (CLA), which may play a role in cancer and diabetes prevention as well as enhanced immune function overall.

Beef Tips
• When possible, purchase beef labeled GRASS-FED or ORGANIC.
• For the leanest cuts, look for the words loin or round in the name. Examples include EYE OF ROUND, TOP ROUND, and TENDERLOIN.
• Select deep red meat, with minimal marbling.
• Trim all visible fat before cooking.
• Always serve a fiber-rich food—such as beans, oats, or fruit—alongside cholesterol-heavy meats. Fiber escorts cholesterol out of the body.

Before grilling beef, marinate it in a thin liquid to infuse flavor and reduce the health risks that accompany high-heat grilling. According to the American Institute for Cancer Research (AICR), marinating meat can reduce formation of potentially carcinogenic HCAs* as much as 92 to 99 percent.

Your Honey's Mustard Sauce/Dip

This improved version of one of America's most popular tangy dipping sauces can be also be used as a salad dressing or for basting meats. The White Bean Puree adds fiber and important nutrients and is a creamy substitute for more than half the fat in a typical honey mustard dressing. This recipe also uses half the honey traditionally found in this beloved dip. If your guy likes it spicy, use a hotter mustard for an extra kick.

MAKES 1 CUP OF SAUCE

4 teaspoons extra-virgin olive oil or walnut oil

¼ cup honey

4 teaspoons cider vinegar

½ cup White Bean Puree (see Make-Ahead Recipe #9)

½ cup Dijon, yellow, or spicy mustard

Salt and freshly ground pepper, to taste

In a medium-size bowl, whisk together the oil, honey, vinegar, White Bean Puree, and mustard. Season with salt and pepper. Cover and store in the refrigerator for up to 3 days.

Sweet and Sour Sauce

anti oxident boost · veggie

Sweet, sour, spicy, and sneaky, this versatile sauce is great over shrimp, chicken, and meatballs.

MAKES ABOUT 1 CUP OF SAUCE

3 tablespoons low-sodium soy sauce

3 tablespoons brown sugar

$\frac{1}{2}$ cup Orange Puree (see Make-Ahead Recipe #2)

$\frac{1}{4}$ cup pomegranate juice

4 teaspoons cider vinegar

$\frac{1}{2}$ to $\frac{3}{4}$ teaspoon cayenne

2 teaspoons ground ginger

Optional extra boost:

$\frac{1}{2}$ cup pineapple chunks

Whisk together the soy sauce, brown sugar, Orange Puree, pomegranate juice, vinegar, cayenne, and ginger. Mix in the pineapple chunks, if using. Cover and store in the refrigerator for up to 3 days.

Sneaky Tip:

Good news for bubble blowers. Researchers have discovered that chewing sugar-free gum all day increases your metabolic rate by about 20 percent, which could burn off more than 10 pounds a year. Chewing gum after a meal also reduces the occurrence of acid reflux.

All-Star Salad Dressings, 3 Ways

Fat-laden salad dressings are often among the first foods sacrificed in the quest for a healthier diet, but who wants to eat a naked salad? With these life-enhancing dressings, loaded with beneficial pomegranate, green tea, and white beans, your man can dress his salad to his heart's content.

Pomegranate Vinaigrette

MAKES ABOUT ³/₄ CUPS OF DRESSING

¼ cup pomegranate juice

2 tablespoons balsamic vinegar

2 teaspoons Dijon or coarse-grain mustard

¼ cup extra-virgin olive oil or walnut oil

Salt and freshly ground pepper, to taste

Optional extra boost: **1–2 chopped garlic cloves or shallots**

In a medium-size bowl, whisk together the pomegranate juice, vinegar, mustard, and garlic or shallots, if using. While whisking, slowly drizzle in the oil. Season with salt and pepper. Cover and store in the refrigerator for up to 3 days.

Green Tea Vinaigrette

MAKES ABOUT ¾ CUPS OF DRESSING

1 green tea bag

2 tablespoons red wine vinegar

2 teaspoons Dijon or coarse-grain mustard

¼ cup extra-virgin olive oil or walnut oil

Salt and freshly ground pepper, to taste

Optional extra boost: **1–2 chopped garlic
cloves or shallots**

Steep the tea bag in ½ cup boiling water for 2 minutes (no longer or it will taste bitter). Allow the tea to cool, then whisk a ¼ cup of tea together with the vinegar, mustard, and garlic or shallots, if using. While whisking, slowly drizzle in the oil. Season with salt and pepper. Cover and store in the refrigerator for up to 3 days.

Green Tea and White Bean Creamy Vinaigrette

anti oxident boost · low carb · low sugar · omega 3s · healthy fats · protein boost · veggie

MAKES ABOUT 1 CUP OF DRESSING

1 green tea bag

2 tablespoons red wine vinegar

2 teaspoons Dijon or coarse-grain mustard

$\frac{1}{4}$ cup White Bean Puree (see Make-Ahead Recipe #9)

$\frac{1}{4}$ cup extra-virgin olive oil or walnut oil

Salt and freshly ground pepper, to taste

Optional extra boost: chopped garlic or shallots, to taste

Steep the tea bag in $\frac{1}{2}$ cup boiling water for 2 minutes (no longer or it will taste bitter). Allow the tea to cool, then whisk $\frac{1}{4}$ cup of tea together with the mustard, White Bean Puree, garlic or shallots, if using. While whisking, slowly drizzle in the oil. Season with salt and pepper. Cover and store in the refrigerator for up to 3 days.

Bountiful Blue Cheese Dressing

anti oxident boost · low carb · low sugar · veggie

MAKES ABOUT 1 CUP OF DRESSING

2 tablespoons light mayonnaise

2 tablespoons White Puree (see Make-Ahead Recipe #4)

2 tablespoons part-skim ricotta cheese

1 to 2 garlic cloves, minced

2 tablespoons freshly squeezed lemon juice

$\frac{1}{3}$ cup blue cheese, crumbled

In a medium-size bowl, whisk together the mayonnaise, White Puree, ricotta, garlic, lemon juice, and blue cheese. Cover and store in the refrigerator for up to 3 days.

DINNERS

BARBELL BURGERS

Sneaky Ingredients: Spinach, Blueberries, Oat bran, Tomato

PIZZA PESTO

Sneaky Ingredients:

Spinach

Broccoli

Peas

RADICAL RIBS

Sneaky Ingredients:

Green tea

Tomato

Cauliflower

Zucchini

VULCAN MOLTEN CHOCOLATE CAKE

Sneaky Ingredients: Blueberries, Spinach, Wheat germ

GRILLED CORN BREAD

Sneaky Ingredients: Cauliflower, Zucchini, Wheat germ

BRAWNY BROWNIES

Sneaky Ingredients:
Blueberries
Spinach
Oat bran
Wheat germ

CHOCOLATE-DIPPED STRAWBERRIES

Sneaky Ingredients:
Spinach
Blueberries

CHAMPION CHEESECAKE

Sneaky Ingredients: Tofu, Yogurt, Walnuts, Oat bran, Wheat germ

ONE-AND-ONLY GUACAMOLE (WITH SPICE BOYS CORN CHIPS)

Sneaky Ingredients: Spinach, Broccoli, Peas

CHERRY VANILLA MARTINI

Cherries

BLUEBERRY MARTINI

Blueberries

STRAWBERRY MARTINI

Strawberries

Fearless Fried Chicken

Find yourself a clean bucket or pail, line it with parchment paper, and load it up with this crispy chicken. No one will guess it's oven-fried and coated in whole grain!

MAKES 4 SERVINGS

¼ cup whole grain flour

½ teaspoon salt

2 egg whites

6 tablespoons White or Orange Puree (see Make-Ahead Recipe #4 or #2)

¼ cup Ground Almonds (see Make-Ahead Recipe #14)

¼ cup cornmeal

Pinch to ¼ teaspoon cayenne

½ teaspoon onion powder

½ teaspoon garlic powder

Freshly ground pepper, to taste

4 skinless chicken breast halves, on the bone (about 2 pounds)

Preheat the oven to 425 degrees. Spray a baking sheet with oil.

Combine the flour and salt in a shallow dish or plate. In another shallow dish, beat together the egg whites and the White or Orange Puree and place the mixture next to the flour. In a third shallow bowl or plate, combine the ground almonds, cornmeal, cayenne, onion powder, garlic powder, and freshly ground pepper; mix well.

Dredge the chicken breasts in the flour and shake off the excess. Dip the chicken in the egg mixture, and then in the cornmeal mixture. Press the breading evenly onto all sides of the chicken breasts.

Place the breaded chicken on the prepared baking sheet. Spray the top of the chicken with oil and bake for about 25 minutes. With a spatula, turn the breasts over once, spray with oil, and then return the baking sheet to the oven for another 20 to 25 minutes, until the coating is lightly browned, crisp, and the chicken is cooked through. Goes well with Real Freedom Fries, page 216, and Side of Slaw, page 185.

Quick Fixes for a Manwich®

Each of the boosters below enhances the nutritional profile of America's favorite sloppy joe. In addition, they cut the acidity of the tomato sauce, which may help prevent acid reflux. Each booster has proven to be undetectable in taste and appearance. Any slight change in texture can quickly be reversed by adding more ground turkey or beef to the sauce. Start enhancing your Manwiches® with the smallest recommended amount of just one of the nutritional boosters, and add a little more each time you serve this meal. You can also mix in two or more of the boosters below, up to a total of ½ cup booster per 1 cup of store-bought Manwich® sauce.

EACH OF THE FOLLOWING QUICK FIXES IS FOR 1 CUP OF MANWICH® SLOPPY JOE SAUCE

* 2 to 4 tablespoons White Bean Puree
  (see Make-Ahead Recipe #9)
Follow the instructions on the can, adding the White Bean Puree to the skillet along with the Manwich® sauce. Mix until well blended.

* 2 to 4 tablespoons White Puree
  (see Make-Ahead Recipe #4)
Follow the instructions on the can, adding the White Puree to the skillet along with the Manwich® sauce. Mix until well blended.

* 2 to 4 tablespoons Orange Puree
  (see Make-Ahead Recipe #2)
Follow the instructions on the can, adding the Orange Puree to the skillet along with the Manwich® sauce. Mix until well blended.

* ¼ cup evaporated skim milk
Follow the instructions on the can, adding the evaporated milk to the skillet along with the Manwich® sauce. Mix until well blended.

* 1 to 2 tablespoons oat bran
Follow the instructions on the can, adding the oat bran to the skillet along with the Manwich® sauce. Mix until well blended.

Secret Sesame Chicken

omega 3s · *veggie* · *healthy fats* · *protein boost*

When we want to pig out on a Sunday night with Chinese take-out, we get mounds of deep-fried, sweet-and-sour sesame chicken. Duplicating the flavor and crunch of this outrageously fattening dish was quite a challenge, but after some trial and error I finally came really close with this surprisingly easy-to-make recipe.

MAKES 4 SERVINGS

$1\frac{1}{2}$ cups Sweet and Sour Sauce, page 235

$\frac{1}{2}$ cup sesame seeds

$\frac{1}{8}$ teaspoon salt

Freshly ground pepper, to taste

1 pound boneless, skinless chicken tenders, or boneless, skinless chicken breasts, cut into strips

Preheat the oven to 350 degrees. Spray a 13 x 9-inch glass baking dish with oil. Spread half the sweet and sour sauce on the bottom of the prepared baking dish.

Pour the sesame seeds on a plate, along with the salt and freshly ground pepper. Press the chicken pieces on the plate, coating each piece evenly with sesame seeds. Gently lay the chicken pieces on the baking dish and cover with the remaining sauce. Bake for 25 to 30 minutes; until chicken is cooked through (no need to flip).

Serve over brown rice.

Cold Sesame Noodles

Here's another of my family's Sunday night Chinese take-out favorites, typically reserved for those times when we're indulging in higher-fat foods before starting a diet on Monday morning. I just had to find a way to enjoy the authentic taste of this dish a bit more often, without the guilt. This recipe does just the trick, with less than half the fat of the original!

MAKES 6 SERVINGS

1 tablespoon brown sugar

4 teaspoons toasted sesame oil

3 tablespoons low-sodium soy sauce

$\frac{1}{4}$ cup tahini (sesame paste), well-stirred

1 cup White Puree (see Make-Ahead Recipe #4)

$\frac{1}{4}$ cup rice wine vinegar or cider vinegar

2 to 3 garlic cloves, minced

$\frac{1}{4}$ to $\frac{1}{2}$ teaspoon dried red pepper flakes, to taste

1 pound Asian noodles or thin spaghetti, ideally whole wheat, freshly cooked

Optional extra boost: 3 green onions, thinly sliced; 2 tablespoons toasted sesame seeds; and/or sliced cucumber strips

In a medium-size bowl, whisk together the brown sugar, sesame oil, soy sauce, tahini, White Puree, vinegar, and garlic. Add red pepper flakes to taste.

Put the pasta in a large serving bowl. Spoon the sauce over the pasta, tossing to coat the pasta evenly. Garnish with sliced green onions, cucumber, and sesame seeds, if using. Refrigerate until cool, or feel free to serve it warm.

Sweet and Sour Shrimp

anti oxident boost • omega 3s • healthy fats • protein boost

MAKES 4 SERVINGS

1 pound large shrimp, peeled and deveined

1 tablespoon minced fresh ginger, or $\frac{1}{4}$ teaspoon ground ginger

1 to 2 garlic cloves, minced

1 tablespoon walnut, almond, or canola oil

1 cup Sweet and Sour Sauce, page 235

Sesame seeds, for garnish

Optional extra boost:

1 small red onion, sliced and/or 1 green bell pepper, coarsely chopped

In a large bowl, toss the shrimp with the ginger and garlic (this can be done up to 8 hours ahead, if kept refrigerated).

Heat the oil in a large skillet or wok over moderately high heat until it's hot but not smoking. Add the shrimp and stir-fry for about 2 minutes, until the shrimp turn pink. Remove the shrimp from the skillet and add the onion and pepper, if using. Sauté until they soften, about 5 minutes. Add the shrimp back into the skillet, along with the sweet and sour sauce, mixing to coat evenly. Garnish with a sprinkling of sesame seeds and serve hot over brown rice.

Perfecto Parmigiano

Veal Parm provides the ultimate canvas for creating a Sneaky Chef masterpiece. By upgrading the breading with whole grains, hiding four veggies in the sauce, oven-baking instead of frying, and discreetly cutting back on the fat in the cheese, this typically sinful dish is now a nutritional superstar! Be sure to pound your cutlets very thin for more plate coverage and to give him the illusion of a larger portion.

MAKES 4 SERVINGS

2 tablespoons olive oil

4 veal cutlets (about 1 pound)

$\frac{1}{2}$ teaspoon salt

Freshly ground pepper, to taste

$\frac{1}{2}$ cup whole wheat flour

3 egg whites

$\frac{1}{2}$ cup Green Puree (see Make-Ahead Recipe #3)

$1\frac{1}{2}$ cups Better Breading (see Make-Ahead Recipe #12)

1 cup store-bought tomato sauce, or $1\frac{1}{2}$ cups Mega Marinara Sauce,* page 228

$\frac{1}{2}$ cup Orange or White Puree (see Make-Ahead Recipe #2 or #4)

4 slices part-skim mozzarella or provolone cheese

$\frac{1}{4}$ cup grated Parmesan cheese

If you are using Mega Marinara Sauce, omit the Orange or White Puree called for in this recipe.

Preheat the oven to 375 degrees. Brush a large baking sheet with the oil.

Place each veal cutlet between two sheets of plastic wrap; pound with a mallet or rolling pin until very thin. Sprinkle the veal with the salt and pepper.

Place the flour in a shallow dish or on a plate. In another shallow dish, beat together the egg whites and the Green Puree and set the mixture next to the flour. Put the breading in a third shallow dish or on a plate.

Dredge each piece of veal in the flour and shake off excess. Then dip the veal in the egg mixture, and then in the breading mixture. Press the breading evenly onto both sides of each veal cutlet. Lay on parchment paper and store in the refrigerator for cooking the next day or proceed to cook immediately.

Place the breaded veal on the prepared baking sheet. Spray the top of each cutlet with oil and bake for 10 minutes. With a spatula, turn the pieces over once, spray with oil, and then return the baking sheet to the oven for another 10 minutes. While the veal cooks, mix the tomato sauce and the Orange or White Puree in a medium-size bowl. Remove the veal from the oven and top each cutlet with about ¼ cup of tomato sauce, then cover the sauce with

a slice of mozzarella and a sprinkling of Parmesan. Return to the oven for 5 minutes, until the cheese is lightly browned and bubbly.

Serve with whole wheat spaghetti and marinara sauce.

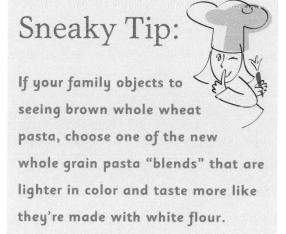

Sneaky Tip:

If your family objects to seeing brown whole wheat pasta, choose one of the new whole grain pasta "blends" that are lighter in color and taste more like they're made with white flour.

Bowling-Night Bolognese

Lure any man home early for dinner with this traditional meat sauce for pasta or lasagna, doctored up with seven sneaky veggies, whole grains, and calcium. And forget simmering for three hours—this sauce tastes just great after just thirty minutes. To make it ultra lean, use ground turkey breast.

MAKES 6 SERVINGS

1 tablespoon extra-virgin olive oil

1 medium-size onion, finely chopped (about 1½ cup)

1 ounce turkey bacon, finely chopped

1 pound lean ground beef or turkey (or mix both), crumbled

3 to 4 garlic cloves, finely minced

¾ cup Green or Orange Puree (see Make-Ahead Recipe #3 or #2)

1 (6-ounce) can tomato paste

1 (28-ounce) can diced tomatoes, with juice

1 cup evaporated skim milk

¼ cup oat bran

½ teaspoon salt

Freshly ground pepper, to taste

Optional extra boost: 1 carrot or celery rib, finely chopped

Heat the oil over medium heat in a deep skillet or earthenware pot. Add the onions and cook until they are slightly translucent, about 10 minutes; add the carrot and celery (if using) and sauté for another 5 minutes. Add the turkey bacon and beef (or turkey), stirring to break it up, and cook for about 5 minutes, until the meat is no longer red. Stir in the garlic, Green or Orange Puree, tomato paste, diced tomatoes, evaporated milk, oat bran, salt, and a few grinds of pepper. Bring to a boil, and then reduce heat to low and simmer for 30 to 45 minutes.

To serve, add cooked pasta of any shape to the pot of sauce and toss to coat every piece well. Top with grated Parmesan or Romano cheese.

Hail Caesar Salad

Sardines are incredibly heart-healthy, but my husband Rick claims to detest the little fishes so much that he'll leave the house if I as much set a can on the counter! Yet every time I manage to sneak sardines into a dish, as in Tricky Tuna Sandwiches, page 172, or Manhattan Clam Chowder, page 198, Rick proclaims it's the best he's ever tasted. In this recipe, I seized the opportunity to hide sardines behind the decoy anchovy flavor customarily found in Caesar dressing, and he's never suspected a thing! Better still, I use green tea to help cut the fat to less than a third of traditional Caesar recipes, and I leave out the raw egg.

MAKES 4 SERVINGS

For the dressing:

1 green tea bag

4 anchovy filets

1 (3- to 4-ounce) can skinless and boneless
   sardines, packed in water, drained

½ cup freshly squeezed lemon juice
   (from about 3 lemons)

1 teaspoon Worcestershire sauce

2 tablespoons red wine vinegar

2 teaspoons Dijon mustard

2 garlic cloves, chopped

½ cup extra-virgin olive oil

½ cup grated Parmesan or Romano cheese

Salt and freshly ground pepper, to taste

For the Parmesan croutons:

3 slices whole grain bread, cut into 1-inch cubes

1 tablespoon grated Parmesan or Romano
   cheese

Salt and freshly ground pepper, to taste

For the salad:

2 large heads romaine lettuce, washed and
   chopped

Grated Parmesan or Romano cheese,
   for garnish

To make the dressing:

Steep the tea bags in $\frac{1}{2}$ cup boiling water for 2 minutes (no longer or it will taste bitter). Allow the tea to cool, then place $\frac{1}{4}$ cup of the tea in the bowl of your food processor, along with the anchovies, sardines, lemon juice, Worcestershire sauce, vinegar, mustard, and garlic. Puree on high until smooth. With the processor running, slowly stream the oil through the processor's feed tube. Add the cheese and puree for another few seconds. Season with salt and freshly ground pepper to taste. Use immediately, or store dressing in the refrigerator for up to 3 days.

To make the croutons:

Preheat the oven to 350 degrees. Spray a baking sheet with oil.

Spread the bread cubes on the prepared baking sheet. Spray the tops of the bread with oil, and sprinkle evenly with the Parmesan or Romano cheese. Season with salt and freshly ground pepper and bake for 15 to 17 minutes, until toasted and golden brown. Cool before tossing into salad.

These croutons can be made 1 day ahead and stored in an airtight container.

To make the salad:

In a large serving bowl, toss the romaine and the croutons with enough dressing to coat all pieces. Garnish with a bit more grated cheese on top.

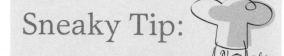

Sneaky Tip:

Here's yet another reason to eat green-leafy veggies: They may help prevent age-related macular degeneration, the leading cause of blindness in older people.

Real Man Meatballs

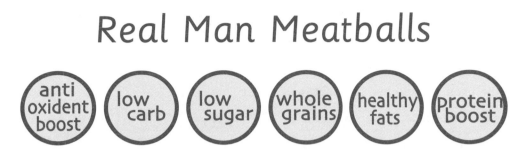

Men and meatballs. What more can I say? Fortunately the color brown is a great cover for our pureed veggies and oat bran. When served with Sneaky Chef tomato sauce you can transform the ordinary into the extraordinary, with a total of eight hidden veggies and whole grains!

MAKES ABOUT 24 LARGE MEATBALLS

1 large egg, beaten

2 to 3 garlic cloves, minced

1 small onion, grated or pureed in a food processor

1 teaspoon dried oregano

1 teaspoon dried basil

$\frac{1}{2}$ cup Green Puree (see Make-Ahead Recipe #3)

3 tablespoons tomato paste

2 tablespoons grated Parmesan cheese

$\frac{1}{2}$ teaspoon salt

$\frac{1}{4}$ cup oat bran

1$\frac{1}{4}$ pounds lean ground beef or turkey

2 tablespoons extra-virgin olive oil, for baking meatballs (or 4 tablespoons for brown-in-pan method)

In a large bowl, whisk together the egg, garlic, onion, oregano, basil, Green Puree, tomato paste, cheese, salt, and oat bran, mixing well with the back of a fork until the green color turns brownish. Add the ground meat and mix with your hands until well combined. Using damp hands, pinch off about 2 tablespoonfuls of the mixture per meatball and gently shape it into golf ball–sized balls.

(Below are two ways to cook the meatballs. The oven-baked method is a lower fat timesaver, and the result is nearly as good as pan-frying.)

Oven-baked method

Preheat the oven to 350 degrees. Brush a large baking sheet with 2 tablespoons of oil.

Gently place the meatballs on the prepared sheet and bake for 10 minutes. Using a spatula to loosen, turn the meatballs over, then return them to the oven for another 10 minutes to brown on the other side. Serve smothered in Mega Marinara Sauce, page 228, either over whole grain spaghetti or as meatball heroes on whole grain rolls or Italian bread.

Brown-in-pan method

Spray a large (10- or 12-inch) nonstick skillet with oil. Place the skillet over moderately high heat, then add 1 tablespoon of the olive oil. Reduce the temperature to medium if the oil starts to smoke. Add the meatballs to the skillet in batches of about 8 to avoid overcrowding. Cook for about 5 minutes, occasionally using two spoons to turn the meatballs so they can brown on all sides. Add more oil to the pan as needed.

To finish cooking through, drop meatballs into a simmering red sauce, such as Mega Marinara Sauce, for 10 minutes. Or preheat the oven to 350 degrees, place the browned meatballs on a baking sheet, and bake for 10 minutes. Serve smothered in Sweet and Sour Sauce, page 235, or cover in tomato sauce and serve over whole grain spaghetti or as meatball

heroes on whole grain rolls or Italian bread.

Sneaky Tip:

Researchers at the Cleveland Clinic are examining the link between low iron intake and male-pattern baldness. According to the study's authors, "Cells use iron to turn food into energy, and it takes a lot of energy to grow hair." Eating iron-rich foods certainly can't hurt!

Doctor's Choice Chili

Chili is one of a Sneaky Chef's best hiding places. As I tested this recipe, I was astonished at the amount of puree that could disappear into this firehouse favorite. I even took some down to the guys at the local station and put them to the Sneaky Chef Challenge. The firemen gobbled up the chili, but none of them could guess the hidden ingredients!

MAKES 6 SERVINGS

1 tablespoon extra-virgin olive oil

1 large onion, minced

1 pound lean ground beef or turkey
   (or a mix of both)

1 to 2 garlic cloves, minced

2 tablespoons chili powder

1 teaspoon ground cumin

$\frac{1}{4}$ teaspoon cayenne, plus additional to taste

Freshly ground pepper, to taste

$\frac{1}{2}$ to 1 cup White Puree (see Make-Ahead
   Recipe #4)

$\frac{1}{2}$ cup Green Puree (see Make-Ahead
   Recipe #3)

1 (6-ounce) can tomato paste

1 (28-ounce) can diced tomatoes

1 (15-ounce) can kidney beans, drained*

1 to 2 cups vegetable broth

Salt, to taste

Green onions, chopped, for garnish (optional)

Low-fat sour cream, for garnish (optional)

Shredded low-fat cheese, for garnish
   (optional)

If your guy objects to whole, visible beans in his chili, simply substitute one cup of White Bean Puree or $\frac{1}{2}$ cup of oat bran for the same nutritious effect.

Heat the oil over medium heat in a chili or soup pot. Add the onion and cook until slightly translucent, about 10 minutes. Add the ground meat, stirring to break it up, and cook until it is no longer red, about 5 minutes. Stir in the garlic, chili powder, cumin, cayenne, and a few grinds of pepper, followed by the White and Green Purees, tomato paste, diced tomatoes, kidney beans, and 1 cup of vegetable broth. Mix well, combining all the colors. Bring to a boil, then reduce the heat to low and simmer for 45 minutes to 1 hour, adding more vegetable broth as needed. Season with salt and more pepper and cayenne, for extra spice.

Sneaky Tip:

Sneaking some White Bean Puree into chili, soup, salad, or your favorite casseroles will help beat the diabetes epidemic. Yale researchers report that eating just half a cup of beans per day can significantly help stave off diabetes.

Top bowls of chili with green onions, sour cream, and cheese, if using. Serve with Grilled Corn Bread, page 294.

Save the leftovers from this meal and put a portion in a thermos or plastic container for your man's lunch.

Vegetarian Variation

Omit the meat and add 2 more cans of pinto and/or kidney beans.

Not His Mother's Meatloaf

anti oxident boost | low sugar | whole grains | protein boost

While it may be hard to compete with his mom's much-loved meatloaf recipe, I'm sure she wouldn't object to your altering her recipe to take better care of her boy. My version of the time-honored turkey meatloaf includes oat bran and white beans as secret fiber boosters.

MAKES 4 SERVINGS

1 large egg

½ cup White Bean Puree (see Make-Ahead Recipe #9)

¼ cup tomato paste

2 teaspoons Worcestershire sauce

1 medium-size onion, diced or pureed (about 1½ cups)

2 garlic cloves, minced

1 cup oat bran

½ teaspoon salt

Freshly ground pepper, to taste

1 pound ground turkey (ideally white meat only)

2 tablespoons ketchup

Preheat the oven to 350 degrees. Spray a baking sheet with oil.

In a large bowl, whisk together the egg, White Bean Puree, tomato paste, and Worcestershire sauce. Mix in the onion, garlic, oat bran, salt, and pepper. Add the ground turkey and mix with your hands until well combined. Transfer the mixture onto the prepared baking sheet and form it into a single rectangular loaf. Glaze the top and sides of the meatloaf with the ketchup, adding a little more if needed to cover the entire loaf. Bake for 50 to 55 minutes, until the internal temperature reaches 160 degrees.

Save leftovers for your man's lunch; put a portion between two slices of whole grain bread and top with tomato slices, onions, or other favorite sandwich fillers.

Potato-crusted Meatloaf Variation

Follow the recipe for Not His Mother's Meatloaf, but omit the ketchup glaze. Cook as directed, but remove the meatloaf from the oven after 40 minutes and spread about ½ cup of leftover Mighty Mashed Potatoes over the top of the meatloaf. Score the top of the potatoes with a fork to create a crispy crust, and finish baking for another 10 to 15 minutes, until the internal temperature is 160 degrees and the potato crust is lightly browned.

Sneaky Tip:

Eat asparagus for washboard abs. Asparagus contains the nutrient asparagine, which helps flush the body of excess fluid and in turn helps to flatten the belly.

BBQ Maximum Meatloaf

This meatloaf is packed with barbecue flavor, a delicious alternative to the usual ketchup-covered meatloaf. I use the kick of the barbecue sauce as a flavor decoy for the Purple Puree.

MAKES 4 SERVINGS

1 large egg

½ cup Purple Puree (see Make-Ahead Recipe #1)

¼ cup tomato paste

¼ cup plus 2 tablespoons barbecue sauce (ideally Homemade BBQ Sauce, page 226)

1 medium-size onion, diced or pureed (about 1½ cups)

1 cup plus 2 tablespoons wheat germ

½ teaspoon salt

Freshly ground pepper, to taste

1 pound lean ground beef

Preheat the oven to 350 degrees. Spray a baking sheet with oil.

In a large bowl, whisk together the egg, Purple Puree, tomato paste, and ¼ cup of the barbecue sauce. Mix in the onion, wheat germ, salt, and pepper. Add the ground beef and mix with your hands until well combined. Transfer the mixture to the prepared baking sheet and form it into a single rectangular loaf. Glaze the top and sides of the loaf with the remaining 2 tablespoons barbecue sauce. Add a little more if needed to cover the entire loaf. Bake for 50 to 55 minutes, until the internal temperature reaches 160 degrees.

Save leftovers for your man's lunch; put a portion between two slices of whole grain bread and top with tomato slices (optional).

Everybody Loves Romano Chicken

Romano chicken is my favorite dish when we go out to eat, so I created this version more suitable for everyday eating, full of sneaky ingredients and oven-baked instead of fried. It's traditionally served with a side of spaghetti with marinara sauce, to which you can add even more of the sneaky purees. This versatile chicken can be served atop a Caesar salad or sliced on a whole grain roll and topped with marinara sauce for a chicken cutlet hero.

I like to double the recipe and store the leftovers, fully cooked, in a plastic bag in the freezer so I can pull a few out to warm up on nights I'm too busy to cook from scratch. Leftovers can be safely frozen for up to three months.

MAKES 4 SERVINGS

$\frac{1}{2}$ cup whole wheat flour

3 egg whites

$\frac{1}{4}$ cup White or Orange Puree
   (see Make-Ahead Recipe #4 or #2)

$\frac{3}{4}$ cup wheat germ

$\frac{1}{2}$ teaspoon salt

Freshly ground pepper, to taste

$\frac{1}{2}$ cup grated Romano or Parmesan cheese

4 boneless, skinless chicken breasts,
   pounded thin (about 1$\frac{1}{2}$ pounds)

Preheat the oven to 400 degrees. Spray a baking sheet with oil.

Place the flour in a shallow dish or plate. In another shallow dish, beat the egg whites together with the White or Orange Puree and set the mixture next to the flour. In a third shallow dish or on a paper plate, combine the wheat germ, salt, pepper, and cheese.

Dredge each piece of chicken in the flour; shake off the excess. Then dip the chicken in the egg mixture, and then in the wheat germ mixture. Press the breading evenly onto both sides of the chicken.

Put the breaded chicken on parchment paper and store in the refrigerator for cooking tomorrow or proceed to cook immediately. Place the breaded chicken on the prepared baking sheet. Spray the top of the chicken with oil and bake for 10 to 12 minutes. With a spatula, turn the cutlets over, spray them with oil, then bake for another 10 to 12 minutes, until chicken is no longer pink. Serve with whole wheat spaghetti and Mega Marinara Sauce, page 228.

Save leftovers for your man's lunch; put a portion between two slices of whole grain bread, or slice chicken and place on a whole grain hero, topped with marinara sauce.

Sneaky Tip:

Consider sharing an entrée on date night— statistics gathered by Penn State University reveal that one regular restaurant portion is the equivalent of three recommended servings!

Fettuccine Don't Be Afraid-O

anti oxident boost · low sugar · omega 3s · veggie · whole grains · healthy fats

Healthy fettuccine Alfredo? Tackling this oxymoron was the ultimate challenge for The Sneaky Chef. Normally loaded with heavy cream, butter, and cheese, it's jokingly referred to as "heart attack on a plate." But with the help of evaporated skim milk and tofu, two of my favorite accomplices, I was able to retain the creamy texture of the original sauce—and a little Parmesan cheese and turkey bacon (or prosciutto) provide the authentic Alfredo flavor!

MAKES 4 SERVINGS

2 tablespoons extra-virgin olive oil

1 tablespoon unbleached white flour

2 cups evaporated skim milk

½ cup (¼ of a 14-ounce block) firm tofu, mashed well or pureed in a food processor

½ cup grated Parmesan or Romano cheese

1 pound fettuccine, ideally whole wheat, cooked according to package directions

2 tablespoons diced prosciutto or turkey bacon bits, for garnish (optional)

¼ teaspoon salt

Freshly ground pepper, to taste

Heat the oil in a saucepan over medium heat. Sprinkle the flour over the oil and stir constantly with a wooden spoon for about 1 minute (this is a *roux*, a fancy name for a thickener). Whisk in the evaporated milk, tofu, and cheese. Reduce the heat to simmer and cook for about 5 minutes, whisking constantly, until the sauce has thickened.

Put the hot fettuccine into a large serving bowl and pour on the sauce, tossing well to coat the pasta evenly. Garnish with the prosciutto or bacon, if using, and season with salt and freshly ground pepper. Serve immediately.

Sneaky Tip:

Prosciutto has all of bacon's flavor, but less of its fat.

Linguine with Red Clam Sauce

anti oxident boost *low sugar* *omega 3s* *healthy fats* *protein boost*

I've secretly added sardines, the world's healthiest fish, to this classic red clam sauce. They enhance the taste as well as the nutritional profile of this dish. But no amount of nagging or statistics on the benefits of sardines' omega-3 rich oils can convince my husband to eat these heart-healthy fish, so I'm extra sneaky when I prepare this recipe. It's always hard for me to hold my tongue as he devours this linguine with red clam sauce!

MAKES 6 SERVINGS

1 tablespoon extra-virgin olive oil

1 medium-size onion, chopped (about 1 cup)

2 to 3 garlic cloves, chopped

½ cup Orange Puree (see Make-Ahead Recipe #2)

3 tablespoons tomato paste

1 (8-ounce) bottle clam juice

1 (28-ounce) can diced tomatoes

2 (6½-ounce) cans chopped clams, drained

1 (3- to 4-ounce) can skinless and boneless
   sardines, packed in water, drained

Salt and freshly ground pepper, to taste

¼ to ½ teaspoon dried red pepper flakes, to taste

1 pound linguine, ideally whole wheat,
   freshly cooked

Heat the oil over medium heat in a deep skillet or earthenware pot. Add the onion and cook until they are slightly translucent, about 5 minutes. Add the garlic, Orange Puree, tomato paste, clam juice, diced tomatoes, and clams. Stir to combine well. Add the sardines, breaking them up with the spoon, slightly mashing into the pot so there are no remaining pieces visible. Bring to a boil, then reduce the heat to medium-low and simmer for 10 to 15 minutes or until the sauce has thickened. Season with salt, freshly ground pepper, and red pepper flakes, to taste.

Add the linguine to the sauce and toss to coat. Transfer to a large serving bowl and serve.

Stuffed Manli-Cotti

This recipe really passes the Sneaky Chef Challenge, thanks to the convenient blandness of high-fiber, low-fat tofu. In this case, the tofu mimics the taste and texture of higher fat cheese. The cheesy mixture also camouflages hidden vegetables, and the tomato sauce affords yet another opportunity to slip in additional undetectable veggies.

MAKES 6 SERVINGS

1 (8-ounce) package manicotti (12 tubes)

1 cup part-skim ricotta cheese

1 cup firm tofu, mashed well or pureed in a food processor ($\frac{1}{2}$ of a 14-ounce block)

1 to 2 garlic cloves, minced

6 tablespoons grated Parmesan or Romano cheese

2 cups White Puree (see Make-Ahead Recipe #4)

$\frac{1}{2}$ teaspoon salt

Freshly ground pepper, to taste

$1\frac{1}{2}$ cups store-bought tomato sauce, or 2 cups Mega Marinara Sauce,* page 228

If you are using Mega Marinara Sauce, omit the White Puree called for in this recipe.

Cook the manicotti according to the package directions. Drain and rinse.

Preheat oven to 350 degrees. Spray the bottom of a 13 x 9-inch baking dish with oil.

In a large bowl, mix the ricotta, tofu, garlic, Parmesan, salt, pepper, and 1 cup of the White Puree. In another bowl, mix the remaining cup of the White Puree into the tomato sauce.

Fill each manicotti with the ricotta mixture, about 3 tablespoons of filling per tube.

Spread $\frac{3}{4}$ cup of tomato sauce on the bottom of the prepared baking dish. Place the filled manicotti in a single layer on top of the sauce. Pour the remaining tomato sauce over the manicotti, cover the pan with foil sprayed with oil, and bake for 30 minutes.

Extra Cheesy Variation

Follow the instructions for Manli-Cotti, but just before baking, sprinkle the top of the casserole with 1 cup shredded part-skim mozzarella cheese (about 3 ounces). Cover with foil and bake as directed. Remove foil for the final 5 to 10 minutes of baking to lightly brown the cheese.

Something's Fishy Sticks

anti oxident boost · low sugar · omega 3s · whole grains · protein boost

These are fish sticks for the adult set—much more exciting to the man in your life than a dainty piece of fish on a plate! The whole grain breading works especially well with the leaner, firmer consistency of wild salmon. You can pan-fry these in a little olive oil, or for a faster, lower-fat option, try oven baking them, as described below.

MAKES 4 SERVINGS

½ cup whole wheat flour

3 egg whites

½ cup Orange or White Puree (see Make-Ahead Recipe #2 or #4)

2 cups Better Breading (see Make-Ahead Recipe #12)

1 pound wild salmon filets, cut into 2-inch strips

Lemon wedges, for serving

Preheat oven to 400 degrees. Spray a baking sheet with oil.

Combine the flour and salt in a shallow dish or on a plate. In another shallow dish, beat the egg whites with the White or Orange Puree; set the mixture next to the flour. Put the Better Breading in a third shallow dish or plate.

Dredge each piece of fish in the flour and shake off the excess. Then dip the fish in the egg mixture, and then in the Better Breading mixture. Press the breading evenly onto both sides of the fish. Lay on parchment paper and cook immediately, or store in the refrigerator for cooking tomorrow.

Place the breaded fish sticks on the prepared baking sheet. Spray the top of the salmon with oil and bake for about 8 minutes. With a spatula, turn the fish over, spray with oil, and return to the oven for another 6 to 8 minutes, until the salmon is cooked through and firm to the touch.

Serve with lemon wedges and Perfect Pesto, page 223, as a dip.

ON THE GRILL

Radical Ribs

What guy doesn't like a nice rack of ribs? While ribs generally aren't considered "health food," you can load 'em up with nutrition by soaking them in an antioxidant-packed marinade, then basting them with my sneaky, low-fat, veggie-packed sauces! Serve with a Side of Slaw, page 185, and Grilled Corn Bread, page 275.

MAKES 4 SERVINGS

1 cup Basic Marinade for Pork, page 231

2 to 3 pounds baby-back pork ribs

Salt and freshly ground pepper, to taste

½ cup Sweet and Sour Sauce, page 235, or Homemade BBQ Sauce, page 226

To marinate:

Pour the marinade into a large zip-top plastic bag, add the ribs, zip tight, and shake. Let the ribs marinate in the refrigerator for at least 1 hour and as long as 24 hours, shaking the bag occasionally.

To grill ribs:

Preheat an outdoor grill to medium. Remove the ribs from the bag; discard the marinade. Season with salt and pepper. Place the ribs on the grill, close the lid, and cook for 25 to 30 minutes, turning occasionally, until they are cooked through. Brush ribs with the sauce and continue cooking for another 10 to 15 minutes, so they are nicely browned and glazed. Cut ribs apart and serve with extra sauce.

To oven-roast ribs:

Preheat the oven to 375 degrees.

Transfer the ribs and marinade from the bag to a 13 x 9-inch glass baking dish, and cook, covered, for 30 minutes, then turn ribs over and continue cooking another 30 to 35 minutes, until they are browned. Brush ribs with the sauce during the last 5 minutes of cooking. Cut ribs apart and serve with extra sauce.

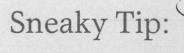

Sneaky Tip:

Incorporating cranberry or pomegranate juice into uncooked foods during food preparation may be a natural way to minimize food-born bacteria.

Charmin' Chicken Parm

As I was testing recipes for this book, I noticed a few extra pounds creeping on, so I cut back on carbs for a few weeks. In order to satisfy my craving for chicken parmigiana, I invented this recipe one night when Rick was grilling plain boneless chicken breasts. It ended up being a family favorite, and no one missed the higher-carb, fried-and-breaded version. Now I even order it this way (though unfortunately without the purees!) when we go out to Italian restaurants.

MAKES 4 SERVINGS

1 cup Basic Marinade for Chicken, page 231

4 boneless, skinless chicken breasts, pounded thin (about 1½ pounds)

1½ cups store-bought tomato sauce, or 2 cups Mega Marinara Sauce,* page 228

½ cup Orange or White Puree (see Make-Ahead Recipe #2 or #4)

¼ cup grated Parmesan cheese

½ cup grated part-skim mozzarella cheese

Salt and freshly ground pepper, to taste

*If you are using Mega Marinara Sauce, omit the Orange or White Puree called for in this recipe.

Put the marinade into a gallon-size zip-top plastic bag, add the chicken, zip tight, and shake. Let the chicken marinate in the refrigerator for at least 1 hour and as long as 24 hours, shaking the bag occasionally.

Preheat an outdoor grill to medium-high, or heat an indoor grill pan to medium-high and spray with oil.

Remove the chicken from the marinade, discard the liquid, and grill the chicken for 3 to 4 minutes per side or until no longer pink inside. Meanwhile, in a medium-size bowl, mix the tomato sauce with the Orange or White Puree.

Preheat the broiler to high. Spread $\frac{3}{4}$ cup of sauce on the bottom of a 13 x 9-inch glass or ceramic baking dish. Lay 2 of the grilled cutlets on top of the sauce, sprinkle with half the grated Parmesan, and then layer the remaining 2 grilled cutlets on top of the Parmesan. Top the chicken with the remaining sauce and sprinkle with the mozzarella and the remaining Parmesan. Broil, uncovered, for 2 to 3 minutes, or until cheese is lightly browned and

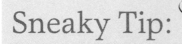

Sneaky Tip:

To keep bugs away from your barbecue and to enjoy eating outside, plant some basil—flies hate it!

Now You're Talkin' Turkey Burgers

anti oxident boost · low sugar · whole grains · protein boost

I served these turkey burgers at our Fourth of July barbecue, and the guys proclaimed them the best turkey burgers in town. My girlfriends and I had a great laugh in the kitchen when I shared my little secret—they are loaded with white beans and oat bran. Freeze a dozen or so, layering them in plastic bags with parchment paper between each burger. With them on hand, you've redefined fast food!

MAKES 4 BURGERS

¼ cup White Bean Puree (see Make-Ahead Recipe #9)

¼ cup oat bran, plus additional as needed

2 teaspoons Worcestershire sauce

½ teaspoon salt

Freshly ground pepper, to taste

1 pound ground turkey (ideally white meat, or a mix of light and dark meat)

4 hamburger buns or English muffins, preferably whole grain

Optional extra boost: lettuce, tomato slices, or grilled onions and mushrooms

Preheat an outdoor grill to medium-high, or heat an indoor grill pan to medium-high and spray with oil.

In a large bowl, mix the White Bean Puree, oat bran, Worcestershire sauce, salt, and pepper. Add the ground turkey, mixing it with your hands until well combined. If it is too sticky, add a bit more oat bran.

Using damp hands, shape the mixture into 4¼-pound patties. At this point, the burgers may be prepared a day ahead and kept covered in the refrigerator or frozen. If you are not freezing for future use, proceed to the next steps.

Spray both sides of the burgers with oil and place them on the prepared grill. Cook for 5 to 7 minutes on each side or until cooked through and no longer pink inside.

Serve on whole grain buns slathered with Perfect Pesto, page 223, or One-and-Only Guacamole, page 300 and optional extras.

Gone Fishin' Salmon Burgers

(anti oxident boost) (low sugar) (omega 3s) (whole grains) (protein boost)

The piece of salmon that goes so nicely on a lady's salad doesn't hold much man appeal, but turn it into a burger, throw it on the grill, and you're sure to have a winner. This recipe is a great way to get your guy to eat more omega-3 protein. The oat bran and hidden veggies are a nice bonus, too.

If you have time, chill these burgers in the refrigerator for an hour before grilling to make them firmer and easier to handle.

MAKES 5 BURGERS

2 egg whites

3 tablespoons freshly squeezed lemon juice (1 lemon)

¼ cup Orange Puree (see Make-Ahead Recipe #2)

½ cup plus 3 tablespoons oat bran

1 teaspoon Old Bay seasoning

1 teaspoon chopped fresh dill, or ½ teaspoon dried

Freshly ground pepper, to taste

12 ounces fresh wild salmon filets, flaked (or 12 ounces canned salmon, drained and flaked)

4 hamburger buns or English muffins, preferably whole grain

Preheat an outdoor grill to medium, or heat an indoor grill pan to medium and spray with oil.

In a large bowl, whisk the egg whites with the lemon juice, Orange Puree, oat bran, Old Bay, fresh dill, and pepper. Add the flaked salmon, mixing with your hands until well combined. If it's too wet, add a bit more oat bran.

Using damp hands, shape mixture into 5 patties. At this point, the burgers may be prepared a day ahead and kept covered in the refrigerator, or frozen. If you are not freezing for future use, proceed to next steps.

Spray both sides of the salmon burgers with oil and place them on the prepared grill. Cook for 4 to 5 minutes on each side, or until cooked through.

Serve on whole grain buns slathered with Perfect Pesto, page 223, or One-and-Only Guacamole, page 300.

Walnut-crusted Variation

Follow the instructions for Gone Fishin' Salmon Burgers, but before cooking, dip the burgers in a shallow dish containing 1 cup of Ground Walnuts (see Make-Ahead Recipe #15).

Sneaky Tip:

To reduce your risk of developing Alzheimer's disease, aim to eat two to three servings of fatty fish each week, limit your intake of saturated and trans fats, and eat leafy greens. Researchers at the Rush Institute for Healthy Aging in Chicago assert that Alzheimer's disease should be considered similar to heart disease, with such factors as diet, exercise, weight, cholesterol, and blood pressure all influencing a person's chances of escaping it later in life.

Grilled Chicken Satay with Peanut Dipping Sauce

One night Rick and I were having dinner with friends in a Thai restaurant, enjoying a decent peanut sauce, and I thought to myself, **what a great opportunity for the Sneaky Chef!** *The next day I went to work invisibly improving this traditional recipe by cutting the fat with hidden Orange Puree and slipping in a bit of oat bran and green tea for good measure. Everyone agreed my new and nutritionally improved peanut sauce tasted even better than the original.*

Taking the time to marinate the chicken first serves a double purpose; even as it infuses flavor and makes the chicken more tender, it cuts the health risks associated with high-heat grilling. For convenience, many of the same ingredients used in the marinade are also in the peanut sauce.

MAKES 4 SERVINGS

1 tablespoon low-sodium soy sauce

Juice from 1 lime

1 tablespoon honey

1 to 2 garlic cloves, minced

1 cup orange or pomegranate juice

1 pound boneless, skinless chicken tenders, or boneless, skinless chicken breasts, cut into strips

Peanut Dipping Sauce (next page)

To marinate:

Pour the soy sauce, lime juice, honey, garlic, and orange or pomegranate juice into a large plastic zip-top bag. Add the chicken tenders, zip tight, and shake. Let the chicken marinate in the refrigerator for at least 1 hour and as long as 24 hours, shaking the bag occasionally.

To make the skewers:

Soak the wooden skewers, one for each chicken tender, in water for about 30 minutes. Preheat an outdoor grill to medium-high, or heat an indoor grill pan to medium-high and spray with oil.

Remove the chicken from the bag, discard the marinade, and push one skewer through the middle of each chicken strip. Cook the chicken skewers on the grill for 3 to 5 minutes per side, or until cooked through. Serve skewers on a platter with a side of Peanut Dipping Sauce.

Peanut Dipping Sauce

MAKES 1 CUP

1 green tea bag

$\frac{1}{4}$ cup peanut butter, ideally crunchy

$\frac{1}{4}$ cup Orange Puree (see Make-Ahead Recipe #2)

2 to 3 garlic cloves, minced

4 teaspoons low-sodium soy sauce

2 teaspoons honey

2 tablespoons freshly squeezed lime juice

2 tablespoons fresh ginger, grated or minced, or $\frac{1}{2}$ teaspoon ground ginger

4 teaspoons oat bran

Hot sauce

Steep the tea bag in $\frac{1}{2}$ cup boiling water for 2 minutes (no longer or it will taste bitter). Allow the tea to cool, then whisk $\frac{1}{4}$ cup of tea with the peanut butter, Orange Puree, garlic, soy sauce, honey, lime juice, ginger, and oat bran. Add hot sauce to taste.

This sauce can be made a day ahead and stored in the refrigerator, though you may need to whisk it again before serving.

Pizza Pesto

anti oxident boost *low sugar* *veggie* *whole grains* *protein boost*

For a colorful (and healthy) change from the traditional tomato sauce pie, try this great use for left-over pesto. This pizza is awesome on the grill, too.

MAKES 1 LARGE PIZZA OR 4 SMALLER PIZZAS

1 bag store-bought pizza dough

¾ cup store-bought pesto sauce, or 1 cup Perfect Pesto,* page 223

¼ cup Green Puree (see Make-Ahead Recipe #3)

1 cup shredded low-fat mozzarella cheese

Optional extra boost:

sliced tomatoes, leftover pieces of roasted chicken, artichoke hearts

*If you are using Perfect Pesto, omit the Green Puree called for in this recipe.

Preheat the oven to 400 degrees. If you are using a pizza stone, preheat it as well, or spray a baking sheet with oil.

Stretch the pizza dough to form desired shape, or use a floured rolling pin to roll out the dough to a ½-inch thickness on a floured surface. Transfer the dough to the prepared pizza stone or baking sheet.

Combine the pesto sauce with the Green Puree. Mix well. Spread the sauce mixture across the prepared pizza dough, then add optional toppings, if using, and cover with the mozzarella. Bake for 15 to 20 minutes, until cheese melts. Allow to cool a few minutes, then cut into triangles and serve.

Grilled Pizza Variation

Preheat an outdoor grill to medium-high. Spray or brush the pizza dough with olive oil. Place the dough on the grill, close the lid, and grill for about 2 minutes. Flip the dough, spray or brush with oil on the other side, and grill for another 2 minutes. Reduce heat to medium-low and spread on the pesto sauce, optional toppings (if using), and cheese. Cook for another 2 to 3 minutes, until the cheese melts.

Pesto Pita Pizza Variation

Follow instructions for Pizza Pesto, but use 4 "Greek style" pocketless pitas (whole wheat preferred) instead of the store-bought pizza dough. Cover each pita with ¼ cup of the sauce mixture and ½ cup of mozzarella cheese.

To make pitas on the grill, follow instructions for the Grilled Pizza Variation.

Sneaky Tip:

Eat pesto to soothe joint pain. In a recent study, basil exhibited the same anti-inflammatory effect as aspirin, but without its harmful side effects. Basil's medicinal properties are tied to the eugenol oil found in the plant.

Barbell Burgers

Taking fat, juicy burgers away from our men isn't an option, but we can help minimize the damage from the saturated fat in the beef with a healthy hidden dose of oat bran fiber, spinach, blueberries, and tomato paste. Secretly pump-up the burgers at your next backyard cookout and enjoy the rave reviews!

If time allows, make the burger patties ahead of time and chill them for an hour before grilling so they're firmer and easier to handle.

MAKES 4 SERVINGS

¼ cup tomato paste

¼ cup Purple Puree (see Make-Ahead Recipe #1)

1/4 cup oat bran, plus additional as needed

2 teaspoons Worcestershire sauce

½ teaspoon salt

1 pound lean ground beef

4 hamburger buns or English muffins, preferably whole grain

Optional extra boost: lettuce, tomato slices, or grilled onions and mushrooms

Preheat an outdoor grill to medium-high, or heat an indoor grill pan to medium-high and spray with oil.

In a large bowl, mix tomato paste, Purple Puree, oat bran, Worcestershire sauce, and salt. Add the ground beef, mixing with your hands until well combined. If the mixture is too sticky, add a bit more oat bran.

Using damp hands, shape mixture into four ¼-pound patties. At this point, the burgers may be prepared a day ahead and kept covered in the refrigerator or frozen. If you are not freezing for future use, proceed to the next steps.

Spray both sides of the burgers with oil and place them on the prepared grill. Cook for 4 to 7 minutes on each side, or to desired doneness.

Serve on whole grain buns slathered with Perfect Pesto, page 223, or One-and-Only Guacamole, page 300, and optional extras.

Grilled Steak

(anti oxident boost) (low carb) (low sugar) (omega 3s) (healthy fats) (protein boost)

MAKES 4 SERVINGS

2 pounds beef tenderloin

1 cup Basic Marinade for Beef, page 232

Freshly ground pepper, to taste

Sneaky Tip:

If you have time to add a step to your cooking, this method for cooking meat is worthwhile. Before putting your meat in the oven, rub it with a little olive oil and sear it in a hot skillet for 2 minutes per side, until you have a nice crust.

Place the tenderloin in a large zip-top plastic bag and pour in the marinade. Zip closed and shake to combine all ingredients. Let the beef marinate in the refrigerator for at least 1 hour and as long as 24 hours, shaking the bag occasionally.

Preheat an outdoor grill to medium-high, or preheat indoor oven to 350 degrees.

Remove the tenderloin from the plastic bag, discard the marinade, and pat the beef with paper towels to dry. Place on a plate (or sprayed baking dish if cooking indoors) and mist with olive oil. Grill meat (or roast in oven) for 12 to 15 minutes or until desired level of doneness. Let meat rest for a few minutes, then slice into fairly thin pieces.

*Serving suggestion: Arrange sliced steak on top of tossed Caesar Salad and season with freshly ground pepper.

Plenty of Polenta

Don't let the word "polenta" scare you into thinking this is a difficult dish to make. In fact, it's very simple to prepare. The only tricky part is to allow it to chill long enough before you attempt to slice and grill it—refrigerate it between four and twenty-four hours first.

MAKES 4 SERVINGS

¾ cup vegetable broth

¼ cup instant polenta*

½ cup White Puree (see Make-Ahead Recipe #4)

¼ teaspoon salt

2 tablespoons Parmesan cheese

*Instant polenta is available at most grocery and natural food stores, sometimes under the name corn grits. If you can't find it, substitute with the same amount of yellow cornmeal and cook for 15 minutes, or according to package directions.

Spray a 13 x 9-inch baking pan with oil. Place a piece of parchment paper on the bottom.

Pour the broth into a large saucepan and bring to a boil. Add the polenta and reduce the heat to low; cook for about 5 minutes, stirring occasionally. Stir in the White Puree, salt, and cheese. Immediately transfer the polenta to the prepared baking pan, cover the pan with foil, and refrigerate until firm, at least 1 hour and as long as 24 hours.

Preheat an outdoor grill to medium-high, or heat an indoor grill pan to medium-high and spray it with oil. Cut the chilled polenta into squares and remove it from the pan. Lightly spray both sides of the polenta squares with oil and grill for 2 to 3 minutes per side, or until grill marks appear on the polenta. Serve warm.

Pizza Polenta Variation

Follow the instructions for Plenty of Polenta, but cut the chilled polenta into triangle-shaped pieces instead of squares and top each piece with one tablespoon marinara sauce (or Mega Marinara Sauce, page 228) and one tablespoon grated Parmesan cheese. Broil until cheese melts, about 1 to 2 minutes.

Love Me Tenderloin

Pork tenderloin is one of the leanest meats available, and because it's nearly as low in saturated fat as chicken breast, it provides a welcome change to the daily dinner menu. Marinating is optional, but as usual, taking this step will tenderize the meat, add flavor, and protect your family from lurking bacteria and the health risks associated with high-heat grilling. The honey mustard glaze tastes equally as good as a nutritious dipping sauce for the meat.

MAKES 4 SERVINGS

1 tablespoon Dijon or
    coarse-grain mustard

Juice from 1 lemon

1 tablespoon honey

1 to 2 garlic cloves, minced

1 cup pomegranate juice

1 pork tenderloin (about
    $1\frac{1}{2}$ –2 pounds)

1 cup Your Honey's
    Mustard Sauce,
    page 228

Freshly ground pepper,
    to taste

To marinate:

Pour the mustard, lemon juice, honey, garlic, and pomegranate juice into a large plastic zip-top bag. Add the tenderloin, zip tight, and shake. Let the tenderloin marinate in the refrigerator for at least 1 hour and as long as 24 hours, shaking the bag occasionally.

To grill:

Preheat an outdoor grill to medium (or preheat an indoor oven to 350 degrees).

Remove the tenderloin from the plastic bag, discard the marinade, and pat the tenderloin with paper towels to dry. Place on a plate (or a sprayed baking dish, if cooking indoors) and slather with ½ cup of the honey mustard sauce. Grill the tenderloin (or roast in the oven) for 35 to 40 minutes or until cooked through to an internal temperature of 155 degrees. Let the meat rest for a few minutes, then slice it into fairly thin pieces. Drizzle the remainder of the honey mustard sauce over the hot tenderloin and season with freshly ground pepper.

Grilled Corn Bread

Corn bread is a no-fail recipe for even the most inexperienced baker. This version upgrades the nutrition with hidden cauliflower, zucchini, and whole grains, and reduces the fat by more than 50 percent.

The jalapeño variation is a great whole grain side dish for barbequed chicken and ribs, and the bacon variation is terrific when served alongside coffee at breakfast. Grilling is an extra step, but it's well worth it for "manly" grill marks and a great barbecued flavor.

MAKES 9 SERVINGS

2 large eggs

$\frac{1}{4}$ cup brown sugar

2 tablespoons extra-virgin olive oil

$\frac{1}{2}$ cup White Puree (see Make-Ahead Recipe #4)

$\frac{1}{2}$ cup fresh or frozen corn kernels*

$\frac{1}{2}$ cup Flour Blend (see Make-Ahead Recipe #13)

$\frac{1}{2}$ cup cornmeal

2 teaspoons baking powder

$\frac{1}{2}$ teaspoon baking soda

$\frac{1}{2}$ teaspoon salt

Optional decoy flavors: $\frac{1}{4}$ cup chopped jalapeño peppers or $\frac{1}{4}$ cup turkey bacon bits

If your man will object to seeing whole kernels, puree the corn in your food processor.

Preheat the oven to 350 degrees. Butter or spray a 12 x 9-inch or 9-inch square baking pan.

In a large bowl, whisk together the eggs and brown sugar until well combined, then whisk in the oil, White Puree, corn, and jalapeño peppers or turkey bacon bits, if using. In another large bowl, whisk together the Flour Blend, cornmeal, baking powder, baking soda, and salt. Fold the wet ingredients into the dry ingredients and mix until flour is just moistened. Bake for 22 to 24 minutes, until the top is light golden brown and a toothpick inserted in the center comes out clean. Let cornbread cool, cut into squares, and remove from pan.

Heat an outdoor grill to medium-high, or heat an indoor grill pan to medium-high and spray it with oil. Lightly spray both sides of each cornbread square with oil and grill for 2 to 3 minutes per side or until grill marks appear on the bread.

HALFTIME SNACKS

Super-Pop Popcorn

Spice up your relationship with a great rental movie and a bowl of this surprisingly healthy and easy-to-make popcorn. Can you believe you can improve your guy's blood circulation just by giving him this delicious snack to munch on? These spices are known to achieve just that! The small amount of sugar gives this a country fair "kettle" corn taste, and you can adjust the amount of heat with the cayenne.

MAKES ABOUT 6 CUPS

$\frac{1}{4}$ teaspoon cinnamon

$\frac{1}{4}$ teaspoon ground ginger

$\frac{1}{8}$ to $\frac{1}{4}$ teaspoon cayenne

$\frac{1}{2}$ teaspoon salt

$\frac{1}{2}$ cup popcorn kernels, for popping

1 tablespoon almond, walnut, or olive oil

1 tablespoon sugar

In a small bowl, combine the cinnamon, ginger, cayenne, and salt.

In a large pot with a lid, heat the oil over medium-high heat. Stir in the spice mixture and the popcorn kernels; mix well. Sprinkle the sugar on top, but don't stir! Reduce the heat to medium, cover the pot, and cook, shaking the pot often, until the popping sound ends. Transfer to a large bowl and serve hot.

Alternative Cooking Method

Sprinkle the sugar and spice mixture over hot microwave or air-popped popcorn.

Sneaky Tip:

Popping two batches of traditional generic popcorn a week, instead of an equivalent amount of microwave popcorn, will save $100 a year.

Spice Boys Corn Chips

anti oxident boost • low sugar • veggie • whole grains • healthy fats

Once you put our sneaky anti-inflammatory spice mix to work on these fast and easy homemade corn chips, you might never buy packaged chips again. These crunchy snacks can be as spicy as you choose, and they provide a good source of calcium, iron, fiber, and all the healthiest spices for men—all for a fraction of the calories and fat of packaged tortilla chips. To keep things interesting, you can easily vary the shapes by cutting strips instead of triangles.

8 DOZEN CHIPS

$\frac{1}{4}$ teaspoon cinnamon

$\frac{1}{4}$ teaspoon ground ginger

Pinch to $\frac{1}{8}$ teaspoon cayenne

$\frac{1}{2}$ teaspoon salt

12 (6-inch) round corn tortillas (white or yellow)

2 tablespoons extra-virgin olive oil

Preheat the oven to 400 degrees.

Combine the cinnamon, ginger, cayenne, and salt in a small bowl.

Brush both sides of each tortilla with oil. Stack 6 of them together and use kitchen shears or scissors to cut the stack into 8 triangles, for a total of 48 chips. Repeat with the remaining 6 tortillas. Scatter the chips in a single layer onto a large baking sheet and sprinkle them evenly with the salt and the spice mixture. Bake 10 minutes, use a wide spatula to flip them, and return them to the oven for another 8 to 10 minutes, until crispy and golden brown.

Serve with Blastin' Bean Dip, page 303, or Heartichoke Dip, page 310.

Chili Spice Variation:

Follow the instructions for Spice Boys Corn Chips, but replace the cinnamon and ginger with equal amounts of chili powder and cumin.

Sneaky Tip:

Spice up your food. Capsaicins—the chemical compound that gives chile peppers their heat. Several recent studies have shown that capsaicin may actually prevent the growth of certain types of cancer.

SNACK IDEAS FOR MONDAY NIGHT FOOTBALL

Almonds, ideally raw, unsalted

Artichoke hearts, whole, packed in water

Carrots, raw, baby

Cherries

Edamame (soybeans), boiled in shell

Grapes

Peanuts, in shell

Pistachios, in shell, ideally unsalted

Pomegranates

Popcorn

Snap peas

Sunflower seeds, in shell

Sweet green peas, in shell

Whole roasted chestnuts, in shell

One-and-Only Guacamole

(anti oxident boost) (low carb) (low sugar) (veggie) (healthy fats)

Guacamole is one of the few green health foods that most guys will gladly dip into. In this recipe, the addition of broccoli, spinach, and peas in the Green Puree increases volume while simultaneously turning this snack into a superfood. Feel free to add one or all of the optional extra boosts, which are not only traditional for guacamole, but also add another important layer of nutrients.

MAKES ABOUT 6 APPETIZER SERVINGS

2 ripe avocados

Juice from 1 lime

$\frac{1}{2}$ teaspoon salt

$\frac{1}{4}$ to $\frac{1}{2}$ cup Green Puree (see Make-Ahead Recipe #3)

Optional extra boost:

$\frac{1}{2}$ cup chopped red onion, chopped tomatoes, handful of chopped cilantro (or fresh basil), and/or chopped jalapeños, to taste

Halve the avocados lengthwise, remove the pit, and scoop out the flesh. In a small bowl, combine the avocado with the lime juice, salt, Green Puree, and the optional extras, if using. Blend lightly with a fork.

Goes well with Spice Boys Corn Chips (Chili Spice Variation), page 299, or Refried Bean Macho Nachos, page 305.

Sneaky Tip:

Cilantro leaves have been found to contain an antibacterial agent that is twice as effective at disintegrating salmonella as the antibiotic gentamicin. The leaves also help detoxify the body, so go ahead and use some in this guac!

Quick Fixes for Store-Bought Guacamole

Each of the quick fixes below not only enhances the nutritional profile of already nutrient-dense guacamole, but the hidden veggies add volume without the fat so your guy can eat even more of this popular dip. Be sure to offer it with smart dipping sticks, such as crunchy celery stalks, carrots, bell peppers, or Spice Boys Corn Chips, page 298. You can also mix in two or more of the boosters below, up to a total of about ¼ cup booster per 1 cup of store-bought guacamole.

EACH OF THE FOLLOWING QUICK FIXES IS FOR 1 CUP OF GUACAMOLE

* 2 to 4 tablespoons Green Puree
(see Make-Ahead Recipe #3)

Combine the Green Puree with store-bought guacamole, mixing until well blended.

* 2 to 4 tablespoons White Bean Puree
(see Make-Ahead Recipe #9)

Combine the White Bean Puree with store-bought guacamole, mixing until well blended.

* 1 to 2 tablespoons oat bran

Combine the oat bran with store-bought guacamole, mixing until well blended. Because of the added texture, this quick fix will go over better if something crunchy, like chopped red onion, is also added in as a distraction.

Chili Macho Nachos

anti oxident boost · low sugar · whole grains · protein boost

MAKES 4 SERVINGS

Large bowl low-fat tortilla chips, ideally Spice Boys Corn Chips (Chili Spice Variation), page 299

2 cups Doctor's Choice Chili, page 261

$\frac{1}{2}$ cup shredded low-fat cheddar cheese

2 tablespoons low-fat sour cream or plain yogurt, for garnish

Chopped jalapeños, to taste, for garnish

Preheat oven to 350 degrees.

Line an ovenproof serving bowl or casserole dish with tortilla chips. Spoon the chili over the chips. Top with cheese and bake for 10 minutes or until the chili is warmed through and the cheese melts. Garnish with sour cream or yogurt and jalapeños. Serve warm.

Sneaky Tip:

Studies show that you will eat 70 percent more food when watching TV than otherwise. Also, overexposure to the bright light of the TV screen decreases your production of melatonin, the hormone that regulates normal sleep patterns.

Blastin' Bean Dip

Refried beans can be a Sneaky Chef's best friend if they are low-fat and made without lard. Pinto beans top the antioxidant and fiber charts, so they're already healthy in their own right—but they also provide a brilliant disguise for our White Puree. And don't discount the health factor of salsa, which is one of the healthiest of America's favorite toppings.

1 tablespoon extra-virgin olive oil

1 small onion, diced (about 1 cup)

1 to 2 garlic cloves, minced

1 cup White Puree (see Make-Ahead Recipe #4)

1 teaspoon chili powder

½ teaspoon cumin

1 (15-ounce) can refried pinto beans, ideally low-fat

1 cup store-bought salsa

Salt and freshly ground pepper, to taste

Optional toppings: Handful of chopped jalapeños, plain yogurt, chopped fresh cilantro leaves, shredded low-fat cheddar cheese, or a dollop of One-and-Only Guacamole, page 300

Heat the oil in a medium-size saucepan over medium heat. Add the onions and sauté until they are slightly translucent, about 10 minutes, and then add the garlic, White Puree, chili powder, cumin, refried beans, and salsa. Stir well to combine, reduce the heat to medium-low, and cook for 10 minutes.

Serve with optional toppings and Spice Boys Corn Chips, page 298, whole grain tortilla chips, or carrot and celery sticks.

Sneaky Tip:

Grumpy frequent flyer alert! U.K. medical journal *The Lancet* reviewed more than five hundred studies on flying and concluded that frequent travelers are more prone to mood disorders, but that a thirty-minute cardio workout before and after a flight cuts depressive symptoms in half. Running to catch a plane may just be the best thing for you!

Refried Bean Macho Nachos

Nachos are so utterly macho—they're a great snack to serve the guys at halftime. Who would suspect he's getting a "square meal" in these triangular shaped crunchy treats?!

1 (15-ounce) can low-fat refried beans, or 2 cups Blastin' Bean Dip,* page 303

1 cup White Puree (see Make-Ahead Recipe #4)

1 cup salsa

Large bowl low-fat tortilla chips, ideally Spice Boys Corn Chips (Chili Spice Variation), page 299

½ cup shredded low-fat cheddar cheese

2 tablespoons low-fat sour cream or plain yogurt, for garnish

Chopped jalapeños, to taste, for garnish

*If you are using Blastin' Bean Dip, omit the White Puree and salsa called for in this recipe.

Preheat the oven to 350 degrees.

Combine the refried beans, White Puree, and salsa in a bowl and mix well. Line an oven-proof serving bowl or casserole dish with tortilla chips. Spoon the bean dip over the chips. Top with cheese and bake for 10 minutes or until bean dip is warmed through and cheese melts. Garnish with sour cream or yogurt and jalapeños. Serve warm.

Super Bowl of Nuts

anti oxident boost · omega 3s · veggie · healthy fats · protein boost

Crunchy, spicy, sweet, and satisfying, this super bowl of walnuts will keep his heart going strong, with beneficial omega-3 oils and anti-inflammatory spices that happen to taste just as good as they are good for him. These nuts are great for munching during a ball game or for tossing on top of a salad or soup.

MAKES 3 CUPS OF NUTS

½ teaspoon cinnamon

½ teaspoon ground ginger

⅛ to ¼ teaspoon cayenne

½ teaspoon salt

2 tablespoons sugar

3 cups walnuts, shelled and unsalted

2 tablespoons almond or walnut oil

1 tablespoon water

Combine the cinnamon, ginger, cayenne, salt, and sugar in a small bowl.

Toast the walnuts in a dry skillet over medium heat, stirring often, until nuts begin to brown, about 3 minutes. Reduce the heat to low, add the oil, and stir to coat all nuts, about 1 minute. Add the spice mixture, then the water, and cook, stirring often, until walnuts are evenly coated, about 5 minutes. Transfer the nuts to a plate and let them cool before serving. Store in an airtight container.

Chili Spice Variation

Follow the instructions above for Super Bowl of Nuts, but replace the cinnamon and ginger with equal amounts of chili powder and cumin.

"No man in the world has more courage than the man who can stop after eating one peanut."

—*Channing Pollock*

Spiced Rattle Snacks

Roasted chickpeas are a popular snack in low-carb diets. Borrowing from that philosophy, I've added our favorite "man spices" to entice guys to crunch on this high-fiber, high-protein snack rather than high-fat chips.

MAKES ABOUT 2 SERVINGS

¼ teaspoon cinnamon

¼ teaspoon ground ginger

Pinch to ⅛ teaspoon cayenne

½ teaspoon salt

1 tablespoon sugar

1 (15-ounce) can chickpeas, drained and rinsed

Preheat oven to 350 degrees.

Combine the cinnamon, ginger, cayenne, salt, and sugar in a large bowl. Add the chickpeas, and toss until well coated. Spread the chickpeas on an ungreased cookie sheet and bake for 55 to 60 minutes, shaking the sheet and mixing occasionally until the chickpeas are crisp and "rattle" on the pan.

Sneaky Tip:

Here's something you probably won't have to nag your man to do. A Greek study suggests that taking a daily afternoon nap may reduce the risk of dying from heart disease by more than 30 percent, which may account for the low level of heart disease in Mediterranean countries where *siestas* are common.

Hungry-Man Hummus

anti oxident boost · low carb · low sugar · omega 3s · healthy fats · protein boost · veggie

Hidden tofu does double duty in this classic hummus dip, cutting fat and adding a boost of nutrients. With the added veggies, this hummus can act as a meal in itself when paired with Spice Boys Corn Chips, page 298, baked potato chips, crunchy stick veggies, or toasted pita bread, or store-bought whole grain tortilla chips. Pair this dip with a Greek salad and you'll have a romantic meal that's fit for a Greek god.

MAKES 4 APPETIZER SERVINGS

1 cup (½ a 14-ounce block) firm tofu, chopped

1 cup canned chickpeas, drained and rinsed

3 tablespoons freshly squeezed lemon juice (1 lemon)

¼ cup tahini (sesame paste)

¼ cup White Puree (see Make-Ahead Recipe #4)

1 to 2 garlic cloves, peeled

½ teaspoon salt

Freshly ground pepper, to taste

Optional decoys: **cayenne, chipotle peppers in adobo sauce, or kalamata olives, to taste**

Steam, boil, or microwave the tofu in water for 2 minutes. Place the cooked tofu in the bowl of a food processor, along with the chickpeas, lemon juice, tahini, White Puree (or optional decoys), garlic, salt, and pepper. Puree on high until smooth.

Serve with Spice Boys Corn Chips, page 298, whole wheat pita triangles, or cucumber rounds.

Heartichoke Dip

I'm not sure what it is about guys and dips, especially hot dips, but they love them almost as much as kids love finger food. Hot artichoke dip seems sinful, and it usually is—it's typically loaded with saturated fat from mayo and cheese. But here the White Bean Puree works overtime, cutting more than half the fat of the traditional dip while simultaneously adding a good dose of fiber and nutrients. And don't discount the benefits of the common canned artichoke heart: this pantry staple is top-rated for antioxidants among all veggies. I've served this dip at a few Super Bowl parties, and it was gobbled up before kick-off!

MAKES ABOUT 4 APPETIZER SERVINGS

1 (14-ounce) can artichoke hearts, packed in water, drained, and coarsely chopped

3 tablespoons light mayonnaise

½ cup White Bean Puree (see Make-Ahead Recipe #9)

¼ cup plus 2 tablespoons grated Parmesan cheese

½ teaspoon onion powder

1 tablespoon wheat germ

Salt and freshly ground pepper, to taste

Preheat the oven to 375 degrees.

In a large bowl, combine the artichoke hearts, mayonnaise, White Bean Puree, ¼ cup Parmesan, and the onion powder. Transfer the mixture into an ovenproof soup crock, baking dish, or large ramekin, and sprinkle the top with the wheat germ and the remaining 2 tablespoons of Parmesan. Bake for 15 to 20 minutes, until the top is bubbly and golden.

Serve hot with Spice Boys Corn Chips, page 298, whole wheat pita triangles, or whole grain crackers.

Hot Artichoke Crab Variation

Follow the instructions for Heartichoke Dip, but add into artichoke mixture ¼ pound fresh lump crabmeat from a refrigerated tin (about 1 cup), drained and picked through for bits of shells. The cooking instructions remain as given.

Sneaky Tip:

Artichokes have long been appreciated as a great source of fiber, potassium, calcium, and iron, but recent research shows that they may also bolster liver function by helping to remove toxins from the body. All that, and they're fun to peel and eat, too!

DRINKS

(NON-ALCOHOLIC)

Fuel-Good Meal Replacement Shakes

In researching men's weight loss programs, I came across a valuable study showing that meal replacement shakes are one of the most effective ways for men to lose 10 to 20 pounds. However, the commercial shakes my tasters tried were unsatisfactory in flavor, texture, and appetite control, so I designed a few of my own sneaky varieties. Each has approximately the same amount of calories, fat, protein, and carbs as the packaged versions, but with much less sugar per serving. They also feature considerably more health-promoting nutrients—you won't find these fresh ingredients in your average canned shake!

There are four flavors here to suit different tastes and to keep things interesting. Best used for breakfast or lunch; drink one serving to replace one meal per day.

Chocolate-Banana Flavor

anti oxident boost · omega 3s · veggie · healthy fats · protein boost

MAKES 2 (1½-CUP) SERVINGS

1¼ cups skim milk

1 large frozen banana (see Make-Ahead Recipe #11)

¼ ripe avocado

¼ cup (about ⅛ of a 14-ounce block) firm tofu

2 tablespoons unsweetened cocoa

1 tablespoon maple syrup or honey

4 ice cubes

Optional extra boost: ½ teaspoon cinnamon, to help stave off hunger longer

Place the milk, banana, avocado, tofu, cocoa, maple syrup, and ice cubes in a blender. Blend until smooth. Serve in a tall glass with a straw.

Strawberry Flavor

antioxident boost • omega 3s • veggie • healthy fats • protein boost

MAKES 2 (1½-CUP) SERVINGS

1¼ cups skim milk

1 cup frozen strawberries, no syrup or sugar added

¼ ripe avocado

¼ cup (about ⅛ of a 14-ounce block) firm tofu

2 tablespoons unsweetened cocoa

1 tablespoon maple syrup or honey

4 ice cubes

Place the milk, strawberries, avocado, tofu, cocoa, maple syrup, and ice cubes in a blender. Blend until smooth. Serve in a tall glass with a straw.

Peanut Butter and Jelly Flavor

(anti oxident boost) (omega 3s) (veggie) (healthy fats) (protein boost)

MAKES 2 (1½-CUP) SERVINGS

1¼ cups skim milk

1 cup frozen strawberries, no syrup or sugar added

¼ cup (about ⅛ of a 14-ounce block) firm tofu

¼ cup peanut butter

1 tablespoon maple syrup or honey

4 ice cubes

Optional extra boost:

½ teaspoon cinnamon, to help stave off hunger longer

Place the milk, strawberries, tofu, peanut butter, maple syrup, and ice cubes in a blender. Blend until smooth. Serve in a tall glass with a straw.

Sneaky Tip:

A recent study of middle-aged British men reports that the more dairy the men consumed (milk, yogurt, and cheese), the less likely they were to have metabolic syndrome, or increased levels of two or more of the following: blood glucose, insulin, blood fats, body fat, and blood pressure. Researchers hypothesize that calcium and vitamin D play an important role in the body's use of insulin.

Chocolate-Cherry Flavor

MAKES 2 (1½-CUP) SERVINGS

1¼ cups skim milk

1 cup frozen cherries, no syrup or sugar added

¼ ripe avocado

¼ cup (about ⅛ of a 14-ounce block) firm tofu

2 tablespoons unsweetened cocoa

1 tablespoon maple syrup or honey

4 ice cubes

Optional extra boost: ½ teaspoon cinnamon, to help stave off hunger longer

Place the milk, cherries, avocado, tofu, cocoa, maple syrup, and ice cubes in a blender. Blend until smooth. Serve in a tall glass with a straw.

Sneaky Tip:

Dr. Christopher Vasey's research suggests that drinking eight ounces of room-temperature water fifteen minutes before each meal helps you to eat about 104 fewer calories at each meal, or enough to lose about thirty pounds in a year.

Homemade Sports Drink

anti oxident boost veggie

This simple, all-natural sports drink, provided courtesy of the Original Himalayan Crystal Salt Company, is an inexpensive, nutritious substitute for the bottled sports drinks on the market, which are loaded with artificial flavors, colors, and sugar. It's great for a quick energy boost and to replenish fluids after a workout!

MAKES 2 CUPS

5 tablespoons freshly squeezed lime or lemon juice

2 tablespoons honey or maple syrup (or 3 tablespoons agave syrup)

$\frac{1}{4}$ teaspoon Original Himalayan Crystal Salt

$1\frac{1}{2}$ cups of water

Put the lime or lemon juice, honey, salt, and water in a blender or tumbler. Blend or shake well. Serve over ice.

Sneaky Tip:

Agave is the key component of good tequila, but it's also an ideal substitute for sugar and artificial sweeteners. Agave nectar ranges from 25 to 45 percent sweeter than sugar, but it also sports a very low ranking on the glycemic index (the chart that measures how quickly a food raises blood sugar), helping to protect you from diabetes-related problems.

ALCOHOLIC DRINKS

Cherry Vanilla Martini

anti oxident boost

Homemade cherry juice not only makes a deliciously sweet martini, it also provides a good dose of antioxidants and significant nutritional benefits.

MAKES 1 DRINK

2 parts Cherry Juice (see Make-Ahead Recipe #7)

1 part vanilla-flavored vodka

Splash ginger ale or Sprite

Shake all ingredients with ice and strain over a chilled martini glass. Garnish with fresh or frozen cherries.

"A fruit is a vegetable with looks and money. Plus, if you let fruit rot, it turns into wine, something brussels sprouts never do."

—*P.J. O'Rourke*

Bloody Mary, "A Salad in a Glass"

When researching hangover remedies, I came across scores of wives tales, from the Irish remedy of "burying the ailing person up to the neck in moist river sand" to the classic greasy-spoon recipe of bacon and fried eggs. I settled on a more sound and appetizing remedy of replenishing lost nutrients with an enhanced version of a traditional Bloody Mary. Feel free to make this a Virgin Mary if you ran out of vodka the night before!

A funny side note: My friend Sharon's husband, Jeff, considers this (or any Bloody Mary) the equivalent of a salad!

MAKES 4 DRINKS

3 cups tomato juice, ideally low-sodium

2 teaspoons horseradish

2 teaspoons freshly squeezed lemon juice

1 teaspoon Worcestershire sauce

2 teaspoons celery seed

¼ cup White Puree (see Make-Ahead Recipe #4)

1 cup chilled lemon- or pepper-flavored vodka

Hot sauce

Freshly ground pepper, to taste

4 whole celery stalks, for garnish (optional)

In a large bowl, whisk together the tomato juice, horseradish, lemon juice, Worcestershire sauce, celery seed, White Puree, and vodka. Add hot sauce and freshly ground pepper, to taste. Pour into 4 tall glasses and garnish each with a stalk of celery for stirring. Serve over ice.

Frozen Green Tea and Pomegranate "Mangaritas"

Our friends Rob and Andrea returned from a year in Mexico and joined our neighborhood block party one Sunday evening last summer. I was in the midst of formulating Sneaky Chef versions of cocktails and challenged Rob to use concentrated green tea and pomegranate juice in his signature margaritas. Armed with our friend Petra's blender, some ice, fresh limes, and authentic Mexican tequila, he emerged from the kitchen with this incredible drink. Suffice it to say, this was a particularly memorable party!

When you're brewing the green tea, I suggest steeping two tea bags in a cup of boiling water for no longer than two minutes, to keep the tea from tasting bitter.

MAKES 1 DRINK

1 part brewed green tea, cooled

1 part pomegranate juice

1 part freshly squeezed lime juice

1 part Cointreau

2 parts good-quality tequila

Ice

Combine the green tea, pomegranate juice, lime juice, Cointreau, tequila, and ice in a blender until smooth. Serve in chilled margarita glasses.

My Sweetheart-tini

Make your sweetie a heart-healthy martini loaded with antioxidant-rich blueberries or strawberries.

2 parts Blueberry or Strawberry Juice (see Make-Ahead Recipe #6 or #8)

1 part crème de cassis (or another berry-flavored liqueur)

2 parts vodka, preferably blueberry-flavored

Fresh or blueberries strawberry, for garnish

Shake all ingredients with ice and strain over a chilled martini glass. Garnish with a few fresh blueberries or a strawberry on the side of the glass.

Sneaky Tip:

Wine packs two times more flavonoids than grape juice, and the fermentation process used to make the wine helps the body absorb them better. Plus, researchers have found that drinking four to seven glasses of red wine per week can lead to a 54 percent reduction in the risk of developing prostate cancer.

Minty Hot Cocoa

Cuddle him up in front of a warm fire with a mug of this spiked hot cocoa. Incredibly nutritious cherry juice enhances the chocolate's richness, and if you choose the Green Juice option, you'll be truly amazed that you can't taste the spinach at all. Each tablespoon of spinach juice offers the equivalent of eating about a quarter cup of spinach, so you'll feel great about sharing this delicious treat with your guy.

MAKES 2 SERVINGS

2 cups skim milk

1 tablespoon unsweetened cocoa powder

1 tablespoon sugar

Pinch salt

½ cup Cherry Juice or Green Juice (see Make-Ahead Recipe #7 or #5)

½ teaspoon pure vanilla extract

1 ounce crème de menthe (or 2 dashes mint extract, for a virgin hot cocoa)

Mini marshmallows, for garnish (optional)

Whipped cream, for garnish (optional)

Stovetop Method

Combine the milk, cocoa powder, sugar, salt, and the Cherry Juice or Green Juice in a pot and warm over low heat. Stir occasionally, until well combined; turn off heat when the liquid reaches the desired temperature (before boiling). Stir in the vanilla and crème de menthe and serve warm in cappuccino glasses or mugs with optional garnishes.

Microwave Method

Mix the milk, cocoa powder, sugar, and salt in a microwave-safe bowl and heat on high for 30 seconds at a time until liquid reaches the desired temperature. Mix in the Cherry Juice or Green Juice, vanilla, and crème de menthe. Serve warm in mugs with optional toppings.

DESSERTS

Chocolate-Dipped Strawberries

MAKES 6 SERVINGS

½ cup semisweet chocolate chips

¼ cup Purple Puree (see Make-Ahead Recipe #1)

12 long-stemmed strawberries, washed and dried

Ground Almonds or Walnuts (see Make-Ahead Recipe #14 or #15), for garnish (optional)

Grated coconut, for garnish (optional)

Sprinkles, for garnish (optional)

Melt the chocolate chips in a double boiler, a metal bowl over simmering water, or in a microwave, checking every 15 seconds. Stir in the Purple Puree and mix well. Dip three-quarters of each strawberry into the melted chocolate mixture. Let the excess chocolate drip off, then place the strawberry on parchment paper. Immediately sprinkle with chopped nuts, coconut, sprinkles, or other toppings and allow to harden, refrigerating to cool more quickly if desired.

Chocolate-Dipped Pretzel Rods Variation

Follow the instructions for Chocolate-Dipped Strawberries, substituting 12 pretzels rods for the strawberries.

Sneaky Tip:

Chocolate may put you in the mood for romance. It helps release mood-elevating endorphins and is packed with flavonoids that help lower blood pressure.

Brawny Brownies

(anti oxidant boost) (indulge) (omega 3s) (veggie) (whole grains) (healthy fats)

When The Sneaky Chef *first came out, one of the most talked-about recipes was the brownie recipe. Everyone was amazed that no one—neither kids nor adults—could detect the hidden spinach, blueberries, oats, wheat germ, or the missing fat and sugar.*

Here, I've slightly modified my signature recipe by adding a bit more sophisticated flavoring for the adult palate (although that didn't stop my kids from devouring them again!). You can also savor the fact that dark chocolate is the new health food, loaded with antioxidants and credited with the ability to lower blood pressure. Add that to the spinach, blueberries, and whole grains, and you'll see why I call these Brawny Brownies!

MAKES ABOUT 16 BROWNIES

6 tablespoons unsalted butter

5 ounces good-quality dark chocolate (not unsweetened), coarsely chopped (or use $\frac{3}{4}$ cup semi-sweet chocolate chips)

2 large eggs

2 teaspoons pure vanilla extract

$\frac{1}{2}$ cup sugar

$\frac{1}{2}$ cup Purple Puree (see Make-Ahead Recipe #1)

$\frac{1}{4}$ cup plus 2 tablespoons Flour Blend (see Make-Ahead Recipe #13)

$\frac{1}{4}$ cup oat bran

One-half teaspoon cinnamon

1 teaspoon instant coffee powder

1 tablespoon unsweetened cocoa powder

$\frac{1}{4}$ teaspoon salt

Butter or non-stick cooking spray

Optional extra boost: **1 cup chopped walnuts**

Preheat the oven to 350 degrees.

Butter or spray only the bottom, not the sides, of a 13-by- 9-inch or 9-inch square baking pan.

Melt the butter and dark chocolate together in a double boiler or metal bowl over simmering water (or in a microwave, checking every 15 seconds). Remove from heat and allow mixture to cool a bit. Meanwhile, in another bowl, stir together the eggs, vanilla, sugar, and Purple Puree. Combine this purple egg mixture with the cooled chocolate mixture.

In a mixing bowl, stir together Flour Blend, oat bran, cinnamon, coffee powder, cocoa powder, and salt. Add this to the chocolate mixture and blend thoroughly. Mix in the chopped walnuts, if using, then pour the entire mixture into the baking pan.

Bake for 30 to 35 minutes, until a toothpick comes out clean. Allow to cool completely in pan before cutting the brownies and use a plastic or butter knife. Dust with powdered sugar, if desired.

Keeps for a week in the refrigerator, covered tightly.

Sneaky Tip:

Sorry fellas. British scientists found women's heart rates rose 20 percent and their bodies released four times more endorphins when eating dark chocolate than from passionate kissing! Dark chocolate made with at least 65 percent cacao will ensure this success.

Feel-Good Fruit Crisp Topping

anti oxident boost | omega 3s | veggie | whole grains | healthy fats

Traditionally, the only redeeming feature of a classic crisp was the fruit hiding underneath a blanket of butter, brown sugar, and white flour. Here we've cut more than half the sugar and fat, substituted a little good fat in the form of nut oil, and added a generous sprinkling of fiber, grains, and walnuts. Save the leftovers for breakfast—topped with a dollop of yogurt, it's better than your average breakfast cereal!

MAKES ABOUT 2 CUPS

$2/3$ cup rolled oats

$2/3$ cup Flour Blend (see Make-Ahead Recipe #13)

2 tablespoons packed brown sugar (half the sugar of traditional crisp)

$1/3$ cup Ground Walnuts (see Make-Ahead Recipe #15)

$1/2$ teaspoon cinnamon

$1/4$ teaspoon salt

3 tablespoons cold unsalted butter, cut into bits

1 tablespoon walnut or almond oil

In a medium-size bowl, whisk together the oats, Flour Blend, brown sugar, ground walnuts, cinnamon, and salt. Using your fingertips, work the butter and oil into the dry mixture evenly, forming little pea-sized clumps. Refrigerate for use within a day, or proceed to make one of the fruit crisps on the following pages.

Berry Crisp

(anti oxident boost) (omega 3s) (veggie) (whole grains)

MAKES 4 SERVINGS

2 cups frozen blueberries or mixed berries, no sugar or syrup added

2 teaspoons freshly squeezed lemon juice

2 teaspoons sugar

$\frac{1}{2}$ teaspoon cinnamon

2 cups Feel-Good Fruit Crisp Topping, page 328

Low-fat vanilla ice cream or frozen yogurt, for serving (optional)

Preheat the oven to 375 degrees. Spray 4 individual ramekins with oil, or for one large crisp, spray the bottom and sides of a 9-inch square baking dish.

Place the berries in a colander and rinse them under cold water to thaw slightly. Drain. Place the berries, lemon juice, sugar, and cinnamon in a medium-size bowl and mix well. Spoon the fruit mixture evenly into the prepared ramekins, sprinkle about $\frac{1}{2}$ cup of the crisp topping over the fruit in each ramekin, and place the ramekins on a baking sheet. If using a 9-inch baking dish, pour in the fruit mixture and sprinkle on the topping. Bake for 30 to 35 minutes, or until the top is golden brown.

Serve warm, with a small scoop of low-fat vanilla ice cream or frozen yogurt, if desired.

Apple Crisp

(anti oxident boost) (omega 3s) (veggie) (whole grains) (healthy fats)

MAKES 4 SERVINGS

3 apples (about 1½ pounds), peeled and chopped

2 teaspoons freshly squeezed lemon juice

2 teaspoons sugar

½ teaspoon cinnamon

2 cups Feel Good Fruit Crisp Topping, page 328

Low-fat vanilla ice cream or frozen yogurt, for serving (optional)

Preheat the oven to 375 degrees. Spray 4 individual ramekins with oil, or for one large crisp, spray the bottom and sides of a 9-inch square baking dish.

Place the apples, lemon juice, sugar, and cinnamon in a medium-size bowl and mix well. Spoon the fruit mixture evenly into the prepared ramekins, sprinkle about ½ cup of the crisp topping over the fruit in each ramekin, and place the ramekins on a baking sheet. If using a 9-inch baking dish, pour in the fruit mixture and sprinkle on the topping. Bake for 30 to 35 minutes, or until the top is golden brown.

Serve warm, with a small scoop of low-fat vanilla ice cream or frozen yogurt, if desired.

Hi-Fi Pie Crust

This delicious crust packs a nutritional wallop! This crust was designed to resemble the texture of a graham-cracker crust, and the men in my family prefer it to the traditional version. It's a great way to sneak some doctor-ordered fiber and nutrients into your family's diet, and it works well with both sweet and savory fillings.

MAKES 1 PIE OR CHEESECAKE CRUST

6 tablespoons Flour Blend (see Make-Ahead Recipe #13)

6 tablespoons Ground Walnuts (see Make-Ahead Recipe #15)

6 tablespoons oat bran

¼ teaspoon salt

3 tablespoons sugar

½ teaspoon cinnamon

3 tablespoons walnut, almond, or canola oil

Preheat the oven to 350 degrees. Spray a 9-inch pie pan (or for cheesecake, a 9-inch springform pan) with oil.

In a medium-size bowl, combine the Flour Blend, ground walnuts, oat bran, salt, sugar, and cinnamon. Mix in the oil. Press the mixture into the prepared pie pan, prick it a few times with a fork, and bake for 14 to 16 minutes, until golden brown.

Champion Cheesecake

I met the Cheesecake Challenge head on, determined to cut its sky-high fat and sugar by more than half while keeping it just as creamy and smooth as Rick loves it. The existing low-fat versions normally use ricotta cheese, which I found to have a disappointing curdy texture. After weeks of testing, I finally achieved the taste and consistency of a real cheesecake by using a combination of yogurt, tofu, and light cream cheese. When combined with the Hi-Fi Crust, page 331, you're sneaking an abundance of superfoods into your man. After the main recipe, I've included just a few possible variations, but feel free to improvise with your favorite flavors.

MAKES 8 SERVINGS

1 (14-ounce) block firm tofu

8 ounces light cream cheese, at room temperature

1 large egg

3 egg whites

$1\frac{1}{2}$ cups vanilla yogurt

2 teaspoons pure vanilla extract

$\frac{3}{4}$ cup sugar

$\frac{1}{2}$ teaspoon salt

1 prepared Hi-Fi Pie Crust for cheesecake, page 331, cooled

Preheat oven to 350 degrees.

Place the tofu and cream cheese in the bowl of a food processor and puree on high until smooth. If your food processor is large enough, add the egg, egg whites, yogurt, vanilla, sugar, and salt and process for a few more seconds. Alternatively, transfer tofu mixture to a large bowl and whisk in the egg, egg whites, yogurt, vanilla, sugar, and salt.

Pour the cheese mixture over the prepared crust and bake until the center is set, for about 75 minutes. Cool for 15 minutes, then run a knife around the edge of the cheesecake to loosen; remove the side of the pan. Refrigerate at least 3 hours before serving.

Banana Cream Variation

Follow the instructions for Champion Cheesecake, but substitute banana yogurt for the vanilla yogurt.

Chocolate Chip Cheesecake Variation

Follow the instructions for Champion Cheesecake, but add ½ cup semisweet chocolate chips into the cheese mixture.

Cocoa Chocolate Chip Cheesecake Variation

Follow the instructions for Champion Cheesecake, but add ½ teaspoon cinnamon, 2 tablespoons unsweetened cocoa powder, and ½ cup semi-sweet chocolate chips into the cheese mixture.

Vulcan Molten Chocolate Cake

anti oxident boost   indulge   veggie   whole grains

This high-end, soufflé-like, exquisite dessert has French chefs fighting over its pedigree. Imagine their **horreur** *to hear I have used their masterpiece as a hiding ground for sneaky spinach and blueberry puree! Shh—don't tell them, but I also cut out half the fat and sugar!*

MAKES 6 SERVINGS

5 ounces good-quality dark chocolate (not unsweetened), coarsely chopped

3 tablespoons unsalted butter

1 large egg

3 egg whites

1 teaspoon pure vanilla extract

$2/3$ cup sugar

$1/2$ cup Purple Puree (see Make-Ahead Recipe #1)

$1/4$ cup plus 2 tablespoons Flour Blend (see Make-Ahead Recipe #13)

1 teaspoon instant coffee granules

$1/4$ teaspoon salt

Low-fat vanilla ice cream or frozen yogurt, for serving (optional)

Powdered sugar, for dusting (optional)

Preheat the oven to 425 degrees. Spray 6 individual ramekins, custard cups, or muffin tins with oil.

Melt the chocolate and butter in a double boiler, a metal bowl over simmering water, or in a microwave, checking every 15 seconds. Remove from the heat and allow mixture to cool a bit.

Meanwhile, in a large bowl, whisk together the egg, egg whites, vanilla, sugar, and Purple Puree. Put this purple mixture into the bowl of the cooled chocolate mixture. In another large bowl, whisk the Flour Blend with the coffee granules and salt. Add this to the chocolate mixture and blend thoroughly. Place the ramekins on a baking sheet and distribute the mixture evenly among the prepared ramekins. Bake 14 to 16 minutes, until the sides are set (though a toothpick inserted in the center will come out with some batter attached).

Serve as is, in the ramekins, or run a knife around the edges of the cakes and invert onto individual dessert plates Add a small scoop of low-fat vanilla ice cream or frozen yogurt, or a dusting of powdered sugar.

Sneaky Tip:

Recent research found that people who drink more than one soda per day—whether diet or regular—have an increased risk of metabolic syndrome, which increases the risk for heart disease.

Ice Cream, 3 Sneaky Ways

anti oxident boost | veggie

Frozen bananas make a creamy and delicious ice cream base. Your food processor is the only way to puree the frozen bananas without having to add a lot of liquid—and for these small quantities, a three-cup mini food processor works best.

I've come up with some delicious variations below, but feel free to add your own flavorings and mix-ins. Also, these recipes can be quickly converted to a thinner milkshake by adding an extra half a cup of milk to all the variations below, then mixing them in the blender.

EACH VARIATION BELOW MAKES 2 SERVINGS

Mint Chocolate Chip Ice Cream	Toasted Almond Ice Cream
2 frozen bananas, cut in pieces (about 2 cups; see Make-Ahead Recipe #11)	2 frozen bananas, cut in pieces (about 2 cups; see Make-Ahead Recipe #11)
6 tablespoons skim milk	6 tablespoons skim milk
2 teaspoons sugar or honey	2 teaspoons sugar or honey
2 drops mint extract	2 drops almond extract
2 tablespoons semisweet chocolate chips	2 tablespoons toasted slivered almonds
Place all the ingredients in the bowl of a food processor and puree on high. Hold on tight—the first few seconds are a bit rough until the mixture smoothes out.	Place all ingredients in the bowl of a food processor and puree on high. Hold on tight—the first few seconds are a bit rough until the mixture smoothes out.

Chocolate-Covered Strawberry Ice Cream

2 cups frozen strawberries, no syrup or

sugar added

$\frac{1}{2}$ ripe avocado

$\frac{1}{2}$ cup skim milk

2 teaspoons sugar or honey

2 tablespoons semisweet chocolate chips

Place all ingredients in the bowl of a food processor and puree on high. Hold on tight— the first few seconds are a bit rough until the mixture smoothes out.

Acknowledgments

I want to take a moment to acknowledge the people who have helped to bring *The Sneaky Chef* into the kitchens of families around the world. My sneaky family has grown since the first book. It now includes the minds and hearts of many tremendously talented people and it is their commitment to this brand that has made it as successful as it is. Thank you, everyone, for all your support.

I am so appreciative for my incredible publishing team at The Perseus Books Group/Running Press – I see why *Publishers Weekly* named you Publisher of the Year for 2007! CEO David Steinberger, Publisher Jon Anderson, Executive Editor Jennifer Kasius, Associate Publisher Craig Herman, Art Director Bill Jones, Publicist Melissa Appleby, and the entire Running Press team —it is an honor to work with each of you.

I am eternally grateful to my family for all their love, inspiration, and guidance: my loving husband, Rick Lapine, and our incredible daughters, Emily and Samantha;

my mother, for the brilliant help on the nutritional glossary and recipe development; my supportive and lovingfather; my stepmother, Ulla Chase, for brainstorming recipe ideas; my brother, Larry, and sister, Karen, who support me always; to my talented stepdaughter, Rachel Arseneau, for creating the nutritional icons; and Brigitte Chase, Bea Miner, and Elyse Dickie for all their creative input. Special thanks to Jean Bukhan, my wonderful test kitchen manager;

Thank you to my invaluable book consultant, Amanita Rosenbush, whose expertise and advice helps create bestsellers; and to Dr. Lori Mosca of New York-Presbyterian Hospital who wrote the foreword for this book; I am so grateful for the support and guidance of my literary agent, Joelle Delbourgo; savvy talent agent, Amy Voll of First Name Media; brilliant publicists, Alison Hill and Jim DeNuccio of CurrentPR; contributing nutritionist Shoshana Werber, whose insights and information make this book so valuable to the reader; and Bill Liss-Levinson of Castle Connolly for all your support;

The visual look of The Sneaky Chef books is a tribute to the creative talent of food photographer, Jerry Errico, and five-star food stylist, Brian Preston-Campbell; and Kris Weber of A/W Design who created the Sneaky Chef logo.

I am very grateful to the team at *UnitedHealth Group*, for all their support; I'd also like to acknowledge the visionary team at *Morgan Stanley Children's Hospital at New York-Presbyterian* for bringing Sneaky Chef foods into their patients' rooms; and Kim Perry and the *Alliance for a Healthier Generation*, a partnership between the American Heart Association and the William J. Clinton Foundation, for allowing me to contribute Sneaky Chef recipes to schools;

Very special thanks to Chef Daniel Boulud for supporting and inspiring me; to Tina Rosengarten for introducing Sneaky Chef to Morgan Stanley Children's Hospital; to Karen Ganz for guiding the recipe development; and Sharon Hammer for all the creative input. I am so grateful for the love and support of dear friends: Laura Klein, Frank Rimler, Carolyn Kremins, Robert Rosenthal, Risa and Steve Goldberg, Denise Gotsdiner, Andy Clibanoff, Stacey Kornfeld, Abby and Bruce Mendelsohn, Petra Kaufman, Tassos Koumbourlis, Jeff Tamarin,

Robert Sutner, Jackie Geller, Karen Rosenbach, Tom Daniel, and Judy Fox.

Finally, to "Fireman Jack" and the guys at the Larchmont fire house, and all the firemen nationwide who consulted with me on recipe development; and of course my list includes you, the reader, without whom *The Sneaky Chef* could not have blossomed. I appreciate your trust and confidence in bringing me into your home.

Dear Readers,

Thank you for sharing your time with us, and for making *The Sneaky Chef* a part of your life. To share your ideas and comments, and for new recipes, tips, special promotions, and appearance dates, please come visit us at:

www.TheSneakyChef.com

I also invite you to share your experience with this method and your own sneaky ideas by emailing me at **Missy@TheSneakyChef.com**. And you may also send me your funny and interesting home video or CD of any sneaky chef moments—good or bad—and share how your family is doing to:

The Sneaky Chef
PO Box 117
Ardsley on Hudson, NY 10503

As often as possible, I will upload these videos on my website and my viewers can vote on which family will receive free personal coaching from me.

Index

Recipes Listed by Make-Ahead Ingredient